"Ryan has written an important and vital book. He tells his incredible story of a new life in a style that makes for a terrific read. His honesty about his transition is one we don't see often and it's very refreshing. This book not only will help those who are struggling with their gender identity but will also educate the masses on what it means to be transgender and in today's society, this is important. FOUR STARS!!!"

—Larry King
Talk Show Host

"Ryan Sallans is an incredibly brave young man who has written a powerful book. *Second Son* will save lives."

—Dan Savage
Co-Founder, It Gets Better Project

"Ryan Sallans takes his readers on this fantastic, page turning journey about life as a transgender male. As Ryan explores his own gender, he offers insight to the personal struggles and triumphs he faces in order to be true to himself. In a society hesitant to acknowledge this difficult and often confusing topic of gender dysphoria, Sallans should be commended for his honesty, courage, and the ability to make the reader aware of this rarely discussed yet timely topic. Ryan Sallans has written a book that will both educate readers and help others who find themselves facing similar dilemmas."

—Dr. Robi Ludwig
Psychotherapist, TV Commentator and Author

"With *Second Son*, Ryan Sallans tells a heartbreakingly modern American man's story, but a story that is simultaneously as old as human history. In prose as deceptively simple and stark as a Nebraska snowfall, Sallans lays bare the truth of the gender identity conundrum in a way that will resonate with readers far, far beyond the borders of the LGBT community. This is a book for anyone who has ever truly loved or tried to understand another human being—be it their friend, family member, or lover. It's also a book for anyone who has ever asked themselves what is the one essential quality that makes them male or female. I'm richer for having read *Second Son,* and Ryan Sallans is a man to be admired. This is a brave man's story, bravely told."

—Michael Rowe
Lambda Literary Award and Randy Shilts Nonfiction Award-winning author of Looking For Brothers and Other Men's Sons

"Second Son: Transitioning Toward My Destiny, Love and Life pulls you in instantly. Thanks to Ryan's straightforward, accessible style, you can't help but care about him and what he experienced thus far in life. Ryan is open about the positive experiences he has had, but doesn't sugarcoat the stories about those who were less than supportive of him. As the book evolves, we see a range of experiences a transgender individual may face, physically, emotionally and socially.

When treated academically, gender identity can be a complex and even convoluted topic. *Second Son* reminds us simply that life can take a great deal of time or change so quickly; that living your life as you are meant to can be extremely complicated and yet so very simple."

—Elizabeth Schroeder, Ed.D., MSW
   Sexuality Education Expert and Executive Director, Answer

"Take your Leap of Faith and read Ryan Sallans' Leap of Faith... *Second Son: Transitioning Toward My Destiny, Love and Life.* Ryan's memoir about his journey invites us to take on our own personal leaps of faith, uncovering aspects of our own true selves. Even after Ryan has participated with me in thousands of medical, educator and counselor presentations, and appeared with me on *Larry King Live*, he has once again astounded me with his honest, revealing and no holds barred auto-biography. This book will undoubtedly enlighten readers around the world and lend much-needed support within the LGBT community."

—Dr. Marilyn K. Volker, Ed.D.
   Sexologist/Gender Specialist, Miami, Florida

"I couldn't put *Second Son* down; it is a moving and inspiring story of one extraordinary man's journey to be himself and be seen as himself by his family and community in the heartland of America. Ryan Sallans is a gifted writer, speaker, and educator. I highly recommend him to any institution seeking to better understand transgender people and issues."

—Lisa Mottet, Transgender Civil Rights Project Director,
   National Gay and Lesbian Task Force

SECOND SON

Transitioning Toward My Destiny, Love and Life

Second Edition

RYAN K. SALLANS

SECOND SON
Transitioning Toward My Destiny, Love and Life
Second Edition

All the events, circumstances, and people in this autobiography are real. In some rare instances, a name was changed to ensure the privacy of the individual.

Scout Publishing, LLC
P.O. Box 31214
Omaha, NE 68132
scoutpublishingllc.com | ryan@scoutpublishingllc.com

Edited by Stephanie Finnegan
Designed by Erika L. Block
Featuring Photos by Fred Schneider
Drawings by Ryan K. Sallans

PUBLISHER'S CATALOGING-IN-PUBLICATION DATA:

Sallans, Ryan K.

Second Son : transitioning toward my destiny, love and life / Ryan K. Sallans. -- 2nd ed. Omaha : Scout Publishing, c2013.

p. ; cm.

ISBN: 978-0-9895868-2-5
Includes bibliographical references.

Summary: Second Son is a story that intimately explores the transition experience of Ryan Sallans, born Kimberly Ann Sallans. Each chapter pulls the reader through Ryan's transition from infant to child, child to body-obsessed teenage girl, teenage girl to eating-disordered young woman, female to male, daughter to son, and finally a beloved partner to a cherished fiancé. It offers readers a unique glimpse of life and love as lived by a uniquely talented and truth-telling man. This is an autobiography for people who love memoirs, individuals struggling with their gender identity, parents seeking to learn more about their own children, adults seeking inspiration, and for college classrooms (specifically psychology, gender studies, and English).--Publisher.

1. Sallans, Ryan K. 2. Transgender people--Identity. 3. Sex--Psychological aspects. 4. Sex change--Personal narratives. 5. Gender identity. 6. Eating disorders. 7. Coming out (Sexual orientation) 8. Gay and lesbian studies. 9. Autobiography. I. Title.

HQ77.8.S25 S25 2013
306.76--dc23   1308

This book is dedicated to all the people who have struggled to find acceptance in this world, who have lost hope, or who have sadly ended their lives because of an aspect of their identity. It is also dedicated to my Grandma Verna. I miss you, Grams.

Table of Contents

PROLOGUE

FREQUENT FLIERS, FREQUENT QUESTIONS

The airline employee's voice is muffled over the PA system. I look around and see other people gathering in line with their boarding passes in hand. I sling my duffel bag over my shoulder and follow suit. A man standing next to me—young, in his mid-twenties, small framed and well dressed—looks me up and down. It's a look I've learned means I am being cruised, or hit on as some would say. I wasn't hit on by men, or really anyone, before, but now it's a different story. I look back at him and smile before refocusing my attention to the airline employee's announcement.

I'm boarding a plane to another city. After I arrive there and complete my speaking engagement, I'll go to sleep, only to rise and repeat the process again the next day. This is the life of a professional speaker. It's a life made possible by my abilities to face my fears, ask myself questions, and honor my truths. The young man standing next to me doesn't know my story or who I am. He just sees a cute guy. He may assume I was the star quarterback on my high-school football team, the popular guy elected prom king his senior year, and the guy whose parents proudly talk about their successful son. I feel he wouldn't believe me if I told him I struggle with my appearance and still don't know if my parents will ever acknowledge—let alone, talk about—the pride they feel for me, their son. I feel he would be even further shocked if he knew the rest of my story.

We all have secrets and identities we want to keep hidden and tucked away from the outside world. I'm no different in this regard. However, some may consider my secrets more unique. While on the plane, if I were to lean over and tell the young man next to me that I am transgender, he may not believe me, or he may be confused as to what that even means. After we land, if he were to follow me to the university where I will be speaking that night, he will join others in the audience and listen to my story and what being transgender means to me, and what my transition through the use of hormones and surgeries has meant to my relationships, my experiences with love, and my sense of self-worth.

Many people in the audience may have come in not knowing that humans can be born the wrong sex, but through my story they learn that without my transition I would have remained stuck in an identity and body that drained me of my energy and my ability to function fully in society. I may be a cute guy now, but my appearance tormented me as a teenage girl and influenced my imagination as a young woman who believed marrying a man would cure me of all the pain and torment I felt inside, but kept hidden from the outside world. My beliefs led me to many failed attempts at dating and further disgust with how I felt in my body. Before my transition I nearly died from an eating disorder; the only thing that saved me was my inner spirit begging for a chance to live. Through my stumbles and explorations I found the path I needed, the path that finally allowed me to stand tall, feet firmly planted on the ground and ready to move forward.

I travel the nation sharing the story of my transition, but not just one related to my gender. It's a story of my transition from infant to child, child to body-obsessed teenage girl, teenage girl to eating-disordered young woman, female to male, daughter to son, and finally a familiar partner to a passionate lover. The whirlwind that has become my life's history and the journey I find myself being drawn to have allowed me to stand back and watch my male spirit fly.

After hearing my story, audience members may see themselves reflected in me due to the emotions that bond us. We all have different tales and experiences that embody our lives, but as humans there exists for us singularity in what we seek: to love and to be loved.

PART ONE

By age four, I was labeled a tomboy—a label
that made my dad happy, I think.
I became his shadow.
Everywhere he went, I followed.
I wanted to be his helper.
I wanted to be just like him.

—Ryan K. Sallans

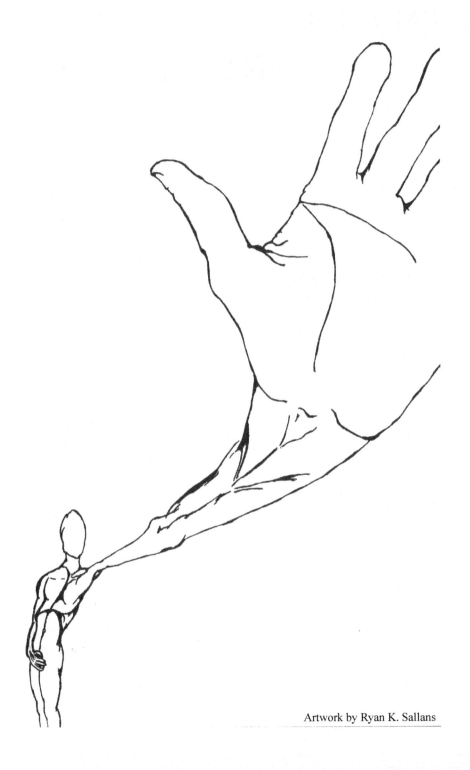

Artwork by Ryan K. Sallans

The needle never really stops intimidating me. I like to pretend that I'm tough, and that it doesn't bother me anymore, but I would be kidding myself.

My ritual with the needle usually happens while I'm sitting on my toilet, with the lid down, of course. My bathroom is small and resides in a house built in 1900. It's a bathroom that was never intended to be in my one-and-a-half–story bungalow house—a home that was built before indoor plumbing was commonplace. Most people refer to it as a "European-style bathroom," which is a nice way of saying, "I don't know how you fit in there." I don't mind its small space, the slanted ceiling that prohibits me from ever putting a shower over the lime green tub, or shelving for towels and toiletries on the sage green walls. I don't mind a place that when it was initially built was not intended to take form the way it has.

While sitting in this space, I look ahead at the tip of the needle and then shift my focus down toward the syringe, where it is attached. Inside the plastic tube is a champagne-like fluid that fills less than an inch of space. My ritual is interrupted when I am startled by my cat Taber's high-pitched meow as she jumps onto the edge of the bathtub; she likes to sit in the bathroom with me. Her green eyes begin to scope out the items I have set out: the prescription bottle filled with an oil-and-testosterone mixture and opened gray and pink packages that held an alcohol swab, needle, and syringe. Taber is intrigued by the packages and quickly grabs one before jumping off her perch and disappearing. I feel less shy when she is gone and no longer looking at me in an inquisitive "what cha doing" way. The bathroom is my private sanctuary; the injection, a spiritual ritual that I don't like to share with others.

I resume my concentration by inspecting my exposed leg; the hair poking through the skin is now thick, long, and dark. I place my pinky finger near the edge of my knee and stretch my fingers across my thigh; they resemble that of a peacock fanning its tail. My skin is cool to the touch, a result of a couple more of my home's quirks: poor air circulation and minimal insulation. My attention flows over the arch of my fingers and lands on my thumb, where I start to envision an imaginary target—a bull's-eye—this will be my desired point of entry.

I inspect where I imagined my target to be on my leg, searching for the faded sign of blue veins running under my skin. If I can dodge the tiny capillaries, then I consider my shot a success; the less pain and bleeding, the better. After injecting in the past, I have worried that I might have hit a vein when a spurt of blood follows the needle as I pull it out, but I really just hit the tiny capillaries, tiny but mighty. My nerves are a little shakier, the closer I get to actually sinking the needle through my skin. I've found that a breathing technique calms my nerves. The scent of fresh Irish Spring bodywash enters my nostrils. It's a smell a girlfriend of mine used to resent because it smelled like a man, a smell that triggered her realization that she couldn't stop my transition; but now she knows it helps to define me. My lungs move in and out while I prepare to move toward the spot that looks most promising.

As I continue the deep-breathing technique, the Irish Spring scent has been replaced by the strong smell of sterilizing alcohol—sharp, defined, and medical. So far, I've injected more than two hundred shots, but I still respond as I did when receiving that first dose more than six years ago: my heart races, my palms sweat, and my hands shake slightly. After a couple more deep breaths, I push the one-inch needle into the top quarter of my outer thigh. The needle sinks through the imaginary bull's-eye I had picked out before; the metal slices through skin, fat, and then muscle. Once the needle can go no farther, I pull back on the plunger and watch large air bubbles fill the chamber. If red doesn't mix with the thick fluid, I push down on the plunger and watch the bubbles leave the syringe. During the injections I sometimes feel relief, other times anxiety. Proper breathing techniques should help; take in a deep breath and then release. I think I keep missing the release part.

The five o'clock shadow that now lines the edges and contours of my neck, chin, and cheeks is almost completely filled in. A strong build now holds up my frame; skin on top of muscle, on top of bone, with some fat mixed in here and there. A voice resonates from my chest through my vocal cords and out into the ears of anyone listening. I've been told my voice partly resembles that of a gay man due to its pitch and intonation. I don't mind if people assume I'm gay; I find comfort in people hearing a male voice and seeing a male body. What they assume my orientation is doesn't matter to me. It's the "T," the nickname for testosterone that brings me this rite of passage; it's the T that may seem daunting and unfair at times, but also makes me feel proud to be who I am.

I engage in this injection ritual every ten days and will continue administering the shots the rest of my life. T will forever be a part of my journey. I believe I'm not less of a man because of how I receive testosterone, even though it would have been easier if I had been born the way my parents had expected over thirty years ago.

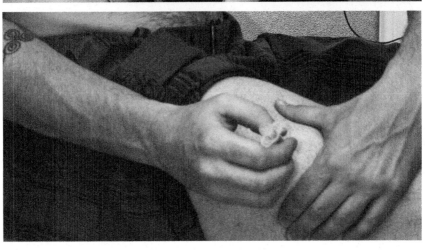

My mom tells me the first time she saw my dad, outside the trailer he was renting next door, the only thing she could think was *What a hood.* At the time she was twenty-three years old and had been pouring a cup of coffee in the kitchen of her two-bedroom house, which she rented with another woman.

"Hood," she said out loud this time as she looked him up and down. He was taking out the trash before getting ready for work that morning. She felt ashamed. Her instinct signaled her to be cautious of him, but her heart put in a few extra beats. A cigarette dangled from under a thick mustache above his lip, which matched the bushy sideburns running up his cheeks. His hair was styled like Elvis Presley, before Elvis converted to wearing jumpsuits. The only thing covering his body was frayed cutoff jean shorts, leaving his deeply tanned skin and well-defined muscles on his broad-shouldered build exposed. Over the summer, before moving to Nebraska, my dad had worked on a road-construction crew in Kansas. A new graduate of the physical anthropology program at the University of Kansas, he was now going to teach biology at the high school where my mom taught home economics.

A few weeks into the school year, my dad gained the reputation of being a good teacher who didn't take any crap from the kids. His ability to intimidate, but not be intimidated, led to a group of "problem" boys, who were called "the dirty dozen," to be assigned to his classroom. My mom, frequently harassed by the popular girls who didn't care about learning how to sew or cook, had the reputation of being a good teacher whom the students could easily make cry. When she saw my dad in the staff lunchroom, the school's hallways, or outside his trailer, it appeared he wasn't interested in her. She didn't know the other male teachers had told him to stay away from her because she was engaged. He didn't know that she wasn't engaged yet, but was expecting a ring for Christmas from her high-school sweetheart. Since my mom wasn't looking for anyone to date, she didn't object when her roommate went out with my dad after one of the school's football games.

After adjusting to the new town and new job, my dad invited a few teachers over to his trailer for dinner and cards; invitees included my mom and her roommate. My dad loved eating home-cooked meals and then playing cards. When he was growing up, card playing was one of the biggest pastimes in his family. After a big meal was finished on Sunday afternoon, it would be customary for the adults to sit around the table on his farmstead in Kansas. His uncle would shuffle through a card deck as they talked, and then would toss the wax-coated pieces of paper around to each seat at the table. The conversations slowed to a few groans or chuckles as they prepared their hands for a game that had been passed down from generation to generation called Sheep's head, or as he says in German, *"Schafe Kopf."* His mother's side of the family emigrated from Germany, so he grew up listening to the intermixing of German with English tossed around the table along with the cards.

As my mom and her roommate made their way across the backyard toward my dad's trailer, they were led by the smell of barbeque ribs. His six-foot frame stood in the entryway, waiting to escort them inside. Before my mom set a woven basket on the table, which contained homemade crescent rolls, she said hello to the other teacher, Jim, who was joining them. When they sat down at the dinner table and began passing around the ribs, corn, and potatoes, the woven basket passed by my dad, who grabbed one of the warm rolls and took a bite.

"Who made these rolls?" he asked.

"I did," a modest voice responded.

He looked over and saw my mom's hand raised; her cheeks were blushing from the attention. He hadn't really looked at her, or saw her as being available, until that moment. He noticed he liked how she wore her brown hair just past her shoulders. Her nose and chin were small, her cheeks were soft and round, and her body was tall and slender. His attraction toward her turned into interest; not only could she bake, but she was also beautiful.

After dinner he asked her to be his partner for cards; she accepted, and they won all hands. My mom's roommate picked up on the vibe between the two of them and knew she wouldn't be going on another date with my dad.

My parents got to know each other more, when my dad offered my mom a ride to an out-of-town teachers' convention two weeks later. To save money, she asked him to drop her off at her parents' house located in a small town just outside where the convention was taking place. After pulling the car up to the old farmhouse, my dad jumped out of the driver's side and grabbed the handle attached to her worn suitcase. He planned to carry it in for her and then drive to his hotel, but instead he ended up spending the next hour chatting with her parents while snacking on some homemade doughnuts her mom had made. Being a true farm boy who fit the saying "the way to a man's heart is through his stomach," he was impressed by both of their baking skills.

Before leaving, he asked my mom for her phone number. He wanted to take her out while they were out of town. She gave it to him, but she was disappointed the next day when he never called. She didn't know he had misplaced that piece of paper and was on the road driving back to her place to ask her out in person.

Being straight out of college in the late 1960s, and new teachers, they were both poor, so they settled on going to a small restaurant, dimly lit and furnished with tiny round tables. My dad was a smoker at the time. When he was in college, he would have a cigarette and a Coke every night while reading in bed. As they waited for their food, he reached into his front pocket and pulled out a soft pack of Marlboro Reds. He pressed his thumb against the sulfur tip of a match and ran it across the rough sandpaper edge of the matchbook. As he moved the lit flame toward the tip of his cigarette, my mom's face scrunched up with disapproval.

A small gray cloud of smoke headed toward where she sat. "I really wish you wouldn't do that," she said.

As the smoke from his first drag left his lungs, he dropped the cigarette into the ashtray and smudged it out. Later that night, after he dropped her off, he vowed to throw out all of the packs that lay in his dresser drawer, quitting cold turkey.

I will always admire him for that; it shows that love can be stronger than any addiction, if you let it.

After their first date my dad went to the local jeweler's to pick out an engagement ring. He pulled out the only money he had in his wallet, fifty dollars, and promised the jeweler he would be back every month to put more money down. The more time my mom was around him, the more she realized that the guy whom she had labeled "a hood" loved to cook, entertain, read books, and spend time with friends and family.

When it came to romance, my dad lived in a world that imitated the movies of his day, where the man is the hero and the protector of the woman. When watching the male characters interact with their buddies, a moviegoer would see them as tough and rugged; but when the camera zoomed in during scenes where the man was alone with the woman, the hero showed his soft and vulnerable side before the screen faded out with a passionate kiss.

My parents-to-be began to spend every evening together; they loved to talk, listen to music, go on walks, and fall into spontaneous actions, like dropping into the winter's snow and making snow angels. To escape from the winter's chill my dad took my mom to the movie *I Love You, Alice B. Toklas.* After it was finished, they returned home where he walked her up to her front step. He waited for her to go inside and turn off the lights before making his way to the snowbank that stood between the sidewalk and the street. The top layer of the snowbank had iced over, creating a frosty shield that a bare finger couldn't penetrate. He noticed a thick branch was sticking out from the bank like a hand reaching for help, the rest covered, not to be revealed until the next melt. He broke off the branch and began to carve out letters in the snow. When my mom woke up the next morning and stepped outside her front door, she felt a rush of warmth over her as she read the etched name, *Alice B. Toklas.* Other people walked by and scratched their heads, unknowing of what was supposed to come before *Alice,* which was *I love you.* My mom had fallen in love, and she knew the feeling was mutual.

Christmas was just a week away when my dad decided it was time to show her the ring he was still making payments on. He lit candles in the living room while they listened to an Andy Williams record, which was rolling out soft melodies. The song "Moon River" began its serenade, prompting my dad to get down on one knee and propose. After two months of dating, they knew they were soul mates, even though forty-three years later my dad still joked that they were on a trial period.

During their engagement they began to talk about starting a family. It was a subject my mom struggled to talk about; she had been told by her gynecologist that she wouldn't be able to have kids, due to her irregular menstrual cycles. This was news that didn't fit into their views of what a family should look like and what they desired. My dad confided in a chiropractor, whom he had begun to see after injuring his back, about the possibility of not being able to have a family. The chiropractor, who worked with a lot of women who had troubles getting pregnant, suggested that my mom come in for an adjustment.

Several adjustments later her periods became regular.

My parents, Paul and Joyce, married in April 1969; four months later they found out my mom was pregnant. After seeing how chiropractic can change lives, my dad applied to school at Palmer Chiropractic. In May 1971, the day they were celebrating my brother's first birthday, they were also driving a car packed full of their personal belongings across the state border toward Davenport, Iowa. For the next three years, my dad balanced any job he could find with going to school. He unwillingly sacrificed time with his family to be able to provide for them. My mom didn't care for Davenport. She hated my dad's long hours, her job as a teacher in a crime-ridden neighborhood, raising my brother mostly alone, struggling with money, and suffering from miscarriages. Although the adjustments had helped her, she was still having problems getting pregnant again. Stress filled their lives, but their love and determination kept them going.

My dad's hard-work ethic was recognized by the professors at the college. As his graduation approached, he was contacted by one of the school's alumni who ran a chiropractic business in Kansas. He had received my dad's name after contacting the school and asking who they would recommend for his practice during the summer while he was away on vacation. Hesitant of moving back to Kansas, my dad decided to accept the offer, he knew after the summer was over he could move on. His dream was to move the family out to Colorado where he could buy a house, with horses, that was nestled in the mountains and adjacent to the sounds of a running stream. He continued to visualize his dream home as he drove the family toward Colorado during their summer vacation. On the way, my dad decided to make a stop in the small city of Grand Island, Nebraska. He had read in the paper that Grand Island was a good place to start up businesses due to the growing population. After driving around the neighborhoods and looking at the business district, both of my parents knew it wasn't where they wanted to live, but before leaving the area, he decided to travel a half an hour east to the small town of Aurora.

Their first impression as they drove into Aurora was charming. The town was populated predominantly by farmers and their families. The business district was built around a four-story brick courthouse and the whole town stretched a mile wide in each direction. It was a town built by farmers and sustained by Christian values and friendly neighbors. When they were visiting Aurora, the people who ran the chamber of commerce treated them like royalty. My dad was impressed by how the businesspeople in town approached him and treated my mom and brother. Their car didn't make it to Colorado; instead, my dad purchased a starter home in a newly developing neighborhood. After the summer had ended, they moved into their new home, and my dad began to build his own practice.

Three years later, my mom was sitting in the bathroom waiting for my dad to come home from work. She had news: she was pregnant again. They anxiously waited for the first eleven weeks to pass before permitting themselves to get excited. They both wanted a big family, so they kept trying. If my mother miscarried this one, it would be number seven. Emotionally and physically exhausted, they decided if this pregnancy didn't take, they wouldn't try again. The eleventh week passed, and twenty-five weeks later, my sister was born. It was 1977.

I was another lucky one, when I arrived in 1979. My parents tried one more time after me, but the pregnancy ended after six months, when my mom had a stillborn. She asked them to take it away; she didn't want to see it or know its sex. After hearing the news, my dad went to his mom's house, where they sat in her bedroom, and he laid his head in her arms and sobbed.

I would be their last child.

When I was born, a second daughter was a bit of a surprise for my parents, who were expecting a baby boy. In the 1970s, ultrasounds were new to the United States and were not as readily available as they are today—especially in rural areas. My parents had let my grandpa use an old wives' tale to help determine my sex. His hard and callused fingers pushed a small piece of thread through the eyelet of a sewing needle, and then pulled the string back toward his chest, where he tied off the two loose ends.

"Give me your right hand; palm open and facing up." My grandpa's voice was gruff from thirty years of chain-smoking. My mom followed his instructions and rested her hand on top of his worn fingers. "Hold still," he said as he gathered up the string and needle and clasped it in his palm before moving it over hers; he then released all but the end of the string. The needle dropped down like a person on a bungee cord that had no spring and began to swing. My grandpa's green eyes watched intently for the dominant swinging direction of the needle before leaning back, looking at my parents and saying, "You're having a boy."

My parents both smiled at the idea of having another boy. My dad had a gut feeling that my brother, Greg, who loved to sing, dance, and draw, wouldn't take much interest in football and other sports. He desired to have a boy like he had been: an all-American sports star. He nurtured this image until the doctor, who guided me out into this world, looked between my legs and exclaimed, "It's a girl!"

The doctor's voice echoed in my parents' ears before it sank in. I wasn't what they had expected. Although my dad was proud to have another child, having another girl smashed the dreams he had set for his unborn son. He left the hospital and drove back to the country, where our new large ranch-style home was located. He walked into the living room, where my grandma, brother, and less-than-enthused sister, Debra, sat on a couch, waiting for the news. "It's a girl," he said before walking away and closing the door to the master bedroom behind him.

The name my dad had originally picked for me was Jarod, which wouldn't work for a little girl. So for the first day in the hospital, my name was "Female Sallans." The next day my brother asked if they could name me "Kim," after his little girlfriend. My parents liked his choice and had "Kimberly Ann" typed across my birth certificate.

When I was brought home from the hospital, the love-hate relationship that grew between my sister and me started the moment my parents left me alone with her in my bedroom. A cry sounded from my lungs; and before my parents could check on me, my sister ran around the corner and proudly proclaimed, "I bit the baby." She was stuck now as the middle child, and her fears of not being the most special one plagued her throughout our childhood.

Photos of me crawling, beginning to walk, and then running around naked after a bath began to join the others in our family's photo album. On the outside we looked like the perfect *Leave It to Beaver* family, but on the inside we struggled, much like any other family. For the most part, our dysfunction remained hidden behind the closed doors of our country home. Arguments that sometimes led to physical and verbal abuse, along with denial of feelings, became common problems within our walls but never made it into the photo albums.

The pressure to fit a certain image drove my family. Having a father who was the primary chiropractor in a close-knit town meant that anything his kids did reflected on his values and his performance as a health care provider. When my dad discovered that my brother was using drugs, which our neighbor's son had given to him, he lost his temper and reverted to actions of aggression toward my brother. My sister harbored a lot of aggression toward me, since I took her place in the spotlight. As I aged, she began to poke at me, pinch me, or call me names, which I reacted to by either hitting or kicking her. She was always a better actor than me, so her fake cries and tattle tales led my mom to spank me with a wooden spoon or my dad to ground me for bad behavior. My parents never knew the right approach to take when they felt like they were losing control of their kids. With each year that passed, they were also becoming frustrated with my growing defiance toward girl clothing and toys. We were raised in a traditional, gender-role household, with manners that matched those roles. My parents taught me manners by reading manuals with such titles as *The Romper Room Do Bee Book of Manners,* by Nancy Claster, from the 1960s.

Her book was lined with messages on how children should behave. My dad or mom would read her book to us at night, "'This is a Do Bee. He's a cheerful, smiling fellow. . . . My name is Bobby . . . I try to be polite . . . from morning till night. . . .'"

We were expected to be a manner-Do-Bee house. However, I never told my parents that when they read the Do-Bee books to me, I would imagine I was Bobby, the polite little boy wearing the nicely tucked-in button-up shirt and trousers, not the Do-Bee girl with her hair in bows, a frilly dress, and lace-fringed socks.

I didn't tell them my desires, but they knew I would cross the lines from what they had believed little girls and boys to be like from the time I was age three. It began when they found my dresses crumpled up and tossed behind my dresser, or when they watched me strip off the top of my two-piece bathing suit so that I could be wearing trunks like my dad and brother. My mom struggled to accept the outfits I would change into while playing in my imaginary worlds. While my sister would prance around the house in her dresses, a purse draped over her arm and lipstick smudged on her face, I would run around in my brother's Cub Scouts shirt or in an outfit made to resemble that of Superman's, with long tube socks pulled above my knees and a dishcloth tied around my neck.

By age four, I was labeled a tomboy—a label that made my dad happy, I think.

I became his shadow.

Everywhere he went, I followed.

I wanted to be his helper.

I wanted to be just like him.

"Faster than a speeding bullet," the announcer's articulate voice bellowed from the TV and into my ears as I sat alone in the family room.

I leaned forward. The warm glow from the wooden box caressed my face.

"More powerful than a locomotive"—his staccato tongue pushed me through the descriptions—"Able to leap tall buildings in a single bound."

I took a deep breath in, to help me puff my chest out, certain that I, too, could leap buildings, once I gained my superpowers.

"Look! Up in the sky! It's a bird. . . . It's a plane. . . . It's Superman!"

My seven-year-old body shot up, off the ground. My right arm lifted above my head as my feet, clad in red-trimmed sweat socks pulled up to my knees, darted me around the room. My idol and mentor, like any other boy's fantasy, was a superhero. My bedroom was filled with homemade costumes, just like those that Martha "Ma" Kent made Superboy. Of course, my "Ma" was my mother, who also crafted a little red skirt to complement the top, but the skirt never left the deep, dark corner of my dresser's bottom drawer. After my dad had taken me to *Superman: The Movie,* I became obsessed. I believed I was like him, a kid who was different, a kid who didn't feel like he fit in, a kid who loved his family and looked up to his dad for advice and his mom for nurturing. My dad and I bonded over Superman. I looked forward to the nighttime storybook readings when he would read the adventures of Superboy to me. I looked at the pictures and imagined what life would be like when I, too, began to obtain my superpowers.

After my dad was done reading, we'd place next to my twin-size bed the books on how Superman came to be. They were perched alongside the one Superman action figure that I had in my possession. I needed only one. His arms moved on joints, his legs bent at the knees, and his red cape, with the yellow *S*, detached from his neck. Whenever Superman was in trouble and needed help, I would detach his red cape and place it on my pinky so that I could then fly in and save him. I imagined myself in Christopher Reeve's role, but my reflection in the mirror always ruined the fantasy. In my reflection I saw that my eyes were green, while his were blue. In my reflection I saw strawberry-blond hair that hung down to my butt; this was not even close to Superman's dark brown hair, which glistened nearly black, with bangs formed into a single curl on the front of his forehead.

No matter how hard I tried to ignore my reflection and move into my imagination, my hair stopped me in my tracks.

That evening my body was sprawled across the lime-green-and-white shag carpet that covered my shoebox-size bedroom. I was playing with a truck made to transport horses, which my grandma had given me. Out of the corner of my eye, I caught my mom's silhouette in the doorway. A muffled tapping began to echo in my room. I looked up to see her rhythmically smack a wooden brush with wire combs against her thigh. Her other hand rested on her hip. For the past five minutes, she had been calling my name from the bathroom, but I had ignored her beckoning.

"Mom, I don't want you to do my hair again tonight," I said. I shifted my attention back to my truck and rolled it under my bed for the night. My bed served as the barn for my animals and trucks.

"We have to. It keeps the tangles out." She stopped tapping the brush and moved through my doorway's threshold. I looked up and saw that there were several brown-colored hair ties wrapped around the wooden brush's handle. My heart sank and gut tightened because I knew that meant she was not only brushing my hair, but pinning it up.

I stayed sprawled on the ground, forcing her to lean over and pick me up. She grunted as she pulled me off the floor and set me down on top of my bed. I was getting too heavy and too old to be picked up.

"I don't know why you don't like this. It's so much easier to do at night than trying to fight the tangles in the morning." Her right hand firmly held a large chunk of my hair near the top of my head as she ran the wires of the brush through it from the top, heading downward. I could feel the pull radiating through my scalp, but I tried not to whine. When I did, she brushed harder—something I don't think she realized.

After she moved through all sections of my hair, she began to part it down the middle and then tightly pulled the pieces together, moving them in and out, and over and under, until they were two long braids on either side of my head. I looked at her face in the full-length mirror that hung on the back of my door. I knew she was concentrating hard on her task at hand. Her lips were curled over her teeth and pursed shut, and her eyebrows increased in their arch as her concentration deepened.

That night was another night she chose to take each braid and roll it up like the string in a yo-yo before pinning the rolls to the side of my head, covering my ears.

"There," she said, proud of another successful night's work.

I turned my attention away from the reflection in my mirror, uncomfortable with how I looked. She ignored my reaction, brushing it off as me being difficult. She leaned over and lifted me off the bed. "Go tell your father good night." She patted me lightly on the butt with the back side of the brush as I headed out of my bedroom and toward the family room, where my dad was watching the evening news.

When he saw me come around the corner, his eyes widened and a smile grew on his face.

"Ah, my little Princess Leia," he said.

I'm not a princess, I thought. I knew exactly what he was going to say. Each night my mom braided and pinned my hair to the sides of my head in a manner that resembled two honey buns, it led to another night of being called a "princess" by my dad. It didn't matter to me that Princess Leia could handle guns, fight and kick butt; the word "princess" overrode any other aspects of her identity to me.

"Good night, Dad," I said while holding back tears. I leaned over the arm of his La-Z-Boy recliner and gave him a kiss on the cheek. I wanted to tell him that I felt uncomfortable and hated my hair, but instead I turned away from him and walked back to my room, heavyhearted. My mom came in to straighten my blankets, a pointless gesture since I only liked one blanket on top of me, and I usually wrapped it around my body to keep all sides warm.

"Good night," she said before kissing me on the forehead.

"Good night, Mom," I said.

"See you tomorrow." She flicked the light switch off as she left my room.

With darkness surrounding me, I began to roll onto my right side, my position of choice, but was stopped by the huge bumper affixed to the side of my head. I turned back onto my back and sighed.

"If I were a boy, I wouldn't have to have long hair," I said to myself before falling asleep, where I could dream about being Superman, with short hair and one large curl running down my forehead.

In two weeks the new school year would begin. I was preparing to enter the second grade and was wondering who would play with me on the playground during recess. The majority of first grade I had hung out with the boys, but by the end of the year, I could tell some of them didn't want me around anymore. I blamed it on my hair and decided I would fix the problem when my mom took me into town for my haircut.

Our old Ranchero pickup, covered more by rust than paint, pulled up to a bright yellow house in town. My mom looked over and saw my sister and me hunkered down on the bench seating, which ran from driver to passenger side. We were embarrassed to be seen in the pickup. My dad had bought it to haul grass clippings and trash to the city dump, but my mom liked to use it for errands.

"Oh, you girls," my mom said as she turned off the ignition, "stop being so silly." She opened her door and looked back at us to make sure we were doing the same.

"I'm just going to stay here," my sister said. She wrapped her arms around her piano books, which she needed for her lessons down the street.

"Okay. I'll be right out," my mom said. She reached out and grabbed my hand as we walked up the stairs and onto the porch, which was covered with Astroturf. My mom lightly knocked on the screen door before opening it up and pushing me in.

"Hello, ladies!" a woman's voice said.

I looked up to see a woman with short red hair, which had been subjected to one too many perms. Her name was Connie, and she always smelled like she had just stepped inside from a smoke break. Her odor was strong and pungent. I wasn't sure if she was a smoker; the strong smells could have been due to a combination of the hair products and perm solutions in her shop, but I never liked going in there and sitting in the stink. I would try to hold my breath, but would stop when I got light-headed.

"Hi," I said to Connie before looking back up at my mom where I waited for her instructions.

She motioned for me to step farther into the shop before saying, "How are you today?"

"Good," Connie replied. "Are we just cutting Kim's hair?"

"Yes. I have to get Debra to piano lessons, so I'll be back in a little bit."

"Okay, see you soon," Connie said. As the screen door closed, the hairstylist looked down at me and asked, "Well, Kim, how are we cutting your hair today?" She plopped me into the chair and wrapped a plastic apron around me.

"Like a boy's!" I exclaimed.

"Like a boy's?" she laughed. "I don't know about that." She pulled my long hair out from under the apron and ran her fingers through it. It was soft and untangled. My mom had spent ten minutes brushing it before we left the house. She was the type of person who wanted things to be presentable. Even on vacations she would have us make the beds before leaving the hotel rooms.

"No, my mom said I could get it cut the way I wanted, and I want it short!" I said.

"Well, okay." Connie took out her scissors and comb. Her left hand wrapped around my hair like she was holding a bouquet. "Are you sure?"

I didn't even have to respond; she could see the excitement in my eyes. The sound of the snipping began, and the hair started to fall.

Enough time had passed before my mom returned that Connie was able to finish my haircut. The first thing I heard after my mom opened the creaky screen door was a gasp. Both Connie and I shot our glances toward her. Still standing in the doorway, she had her right hand over her mouth and her left grasping her chest. When I had entered Connie's house, I had long strawberry-blond hair. After Connie removed the long strands of hair that had been beaten by the sun, the dark roots were exposed. I started to smile, ear to ear, when I noticed my hair was actually brown and now short, resembling that of Superman.

"Are you okay? She s-said you gave her p-permission. . . ." Connie had started to stammer.

"Uh, I'm fine," my mom said. She put her right hand up in the air; her left was still over her chest. "Can we, uh . . . can we have an envelope and keep some of her old hair?"

"Sure," Connie said as she darted over to a drawer that held some of her office items. "She said she wanted it this way," she mumbled.

And I did. . . . I loved it!

The car ride home was quiet, but I didn't mind. In my head I was playing out all of the things that I would do that day, and was excited knowing that I wouldn't have to deal with ponytails, honey buns, morning hair combing, evening hair pulling, and curling irons anymore. I was starting to feel free.

As my mom pulled up to the garage, I barely let the truck roll to a stop before jumping out.

"Kim! I'm not stopped yet!"

I didn't listen to her. I was too busy running around the garage and into the backyard, greeting the breeze, the sun, and the lightness of my head. I ran past our sliding door and caught a glimpse of my reflection. I took a couple steps back and looked myself up and down: blue jeans, a red T-shirt with a Husky pup on it, our elementary school's mascot, and my short brown hair. A warm rush went through my body and I jumped straight up into the air. As I came back down, I turned my head and noticed my dad was on our back porch.

I began running toward him, but quickly slowed my pace when I saw a confused look on his face. It was as if he didn't know who I was, like I was some kid who had just wandered into our backyard and was coming up to ask for directions.

"Kim." He didn't question me but just firmly said my name. I could tell by his facial expressions he wasn't happy with my haircut. "You cut off all your hair. . . ."

I didn't say anything; I didn't know what to say. The disappointment in his voice smashed any excitement I had running through my body and filled it with fear. I feared he would make me go back to the salon and have Connie attempt to glue my hair back onto my head. My parents' reactions left me confused. After I saw my haircut, I finally felt like me; but now with my parents' obvious disapproval, I didn't know if that was okay.

The conversation at the dinner table that night was limited. My dad sat to my left and focused on cutting his steak; my sister was to my right, trying to hide her meat in her napkin; my mom sat across from me, pushing around her peas. Her fork lightly scraped against the plate. I sat there and imagined what it was going to be like to sleep on my right side again, and how it would feel in a few days to jump out of bed in the morning, run a brush through my hair, and then head out the door to go to school.

When the first day of school arrived, I wasn't allowed to run a brush through my hair. Instead, my mom dressed me in a plaid dress, with a white ruffled shirt, and black dress shoes. That morning her lips were pursed and her eyebrows were raised as she tried to curl the edges of my hair so they curled up and away from my neck and ears.

"There," she said. She set the comb and curling iron down and placed her hands on her hips as she looked at me. I looked back at her through the reflection in the mirror and felt a bit deflated. The short hair was there, but the look I had been going for was taken away by curls and hair spray.

Until I was in eighth grade, I was forced to wear a dress to the first day of school.

At age seven I pushed away my fear of being outdoors, alone, at night. It was necessary for me to overcome this fear since I believed stars held the magical powers that would help me, and that wishes directed at them only worked if I was outside.

When I was outside, I noticed that the dark colors running through our country pasture enveloped me faster than the darkness by the house, which was dimly illuminated by lights from the bay window. The pasture grass would wrap around my feet, while crickets chirped in melody with the cicadas in the trees. They all serenaded me as my body swayed back and forth with the shifts of the evening breeze, and my movement became in sync with the tree branches, corn leaves, and tall whisks of prairie grass. Being alone out there was a contradictory experience, an anxious peacefulness. Besides the sounds of nature, I heard nothing—no cars, booming stereos, loud conversations, or sirens. It was my sanctuary, my solace, to make a very personal wish.

"I wish I were a boy," I said to the first star that poked through the darkness. It worked in the movies, so it should work for me now.

My newfound hope and nightly wishes started after watching a movie, *Something Special,* which debuted in 1986. The movie, which is also called *Willy/Milly,* flopped in the theaters; critics hated it and the general public wasn't sure what to think, but to me it was a saving grace.

I happened across it one morning out of chance. Waking up at four-thirty was just a typical Saturday for me, and being unable to lie still and wait for others, I would wander out to our family room and plop myself down next to the fireplace, on top of the orange shag carpet. The draft from the flue always gave me the chills, but it was my favorite place to sit. I stayed warm by wrapping myself up with my blue blanket and hugging my big brown bear. The glow of the old TV and movement of light from the dancing cartoon figures kept me company while the rest of the household was asleep. On this particular morning Gonzo, Little Kermit, and Miss Piggy weren't holding my interest. So I got up and began turning the knob of the TV, waiting with each flip for the image to pull into focus on the screen.

I kept flipping until I landed on HBO. Sometimes an old episode of *Fraggle Rock* would be on, but today it was a movie. I saw a girl on the screen who had the same type of hairstyle as mine; it was brown in color and cut a little above neck length, causing the ends of her hair to curl outward. She was also a tomboy, who liked playing sports; she liked to look at things through a microscope and wore jean shorts and T-shirts. The girl, Milly, was struggling with her parents. They wanted her to act more like a lady, but she wasn't happy with their requests. I watched as she proclaimed to her friends that it would be easier if she were a boy.

The movie pulled me in even further when her best friend's little brother, played by the tiny Seth Green, gave her magic sand and instructions on what to do to make her deepest wish happen. That night she took the sand and drew a circle around herself. She then said a little chant and threw a rock. I watched with anticipation as she went to bed, and then she woke up the next morning, only to notice something different about the way that she walked. She looked down her gray sweatpants and saw that she had a penis. Milly fainted after seeing the change, but I jumped up off the floor and tightly squeezed my big brown teddy bear.

"It's possible!" I told him. "I can be a boy. My body can change!"

Before I saw this movie, I would look at my male friends on the playground and be disappointed that I wasn't just like them. Now I was on a mission to change my body so that I could be a card-carrying member in the boys' club. I began to vocalize some of my wishes around my family and other adults; but while attending a church group, I quickly learned that trusting adults was a mistake.

All of us who attended the church group that night had been given instructions to write a letter to Santa, asking him for a Christmas gift. Placed in front of me on the table was a white piece of paper and a crayon. I picked up my crayon and wrote in my letter, *I would like boy's underwear.* After we were finished, we all ran over to our group leader and handed her our letters. She waited until we all took our seats before pulling out each piece of paper individually and happily reading what each of us wanted. Her face was bright and full of smiles, until she pulled out my white, messily folded letter and began to read over my scribbles. As she read to herself, her smile turned downward. Then she sternly called me up to the front of the room.

"This is not appropriate," she scolded. Her plump fingers tightly squeezed my letter and moved it back and forth in front of me.

I had the reputation of being the ornery kid in the group; nothing I said or did was ever taken seriously. I knew my parents would be told about my behavior, again, and I would then be lectured about what things were appropriate for little girls to do. I hated that church; no one understood me there.

♀

The only people I felt safe with were a handful of friends. There were a couple of girls whom I had crushes on, but I wouldn't tell them. Instead, I would daydream of pulling them into the pasture with me, where I would squeeze their hands and they squeezed mine while we wished as hard as we could that I would be a boy. I imagined swirling sparkles spinning around me while I magically changed in front of them, even though nothing about my appearance would change, only my genitals. After the sparkles disappeared, I believed they would see me and then fall in love with me.

There was one girl who was in the dream with me the most; her name was Megan. She had long, curly red hair; freckles speckled her nose and cheeks. She had a spunky spirit. My friendship with her grew between third and fifth grade. At first, I didn't like her because she was mean to me. We had desks that sat next to each other in our homeroom. Every time I got up to sharpen a pencil or grab a drink of water, she would slam my books shut, causing me to lose my page, or she would push them off the top of my desk, leaving them on the ground for me to find. Every time she did it, I would look over at her and furrow my eyebrows while I scrunched up my face. She would look back and just giggle. After we joined a summer club together with other girls in the community, we started to move past her picking on me.

I was never the loner in school or in clubs, but I always felt stuck between or among identities. Some of my friends were classified as the popular ones; and although I hung out with them, I was never popular. My other friends were the smart ones, but I had a firm belief that I also didn't fit with them, since I spent most of my elementary-school years in special education for reading, writing, and math. I was placed in SPED after my first-grade teachers realized I wasn't as quick a learner as my brother and sister had been. The teachers first started me out in the highest learning group. However, after a couple of days, they asked me to grab my pencil box and move to the next group. I was there for another day before being moved again. Finally I was asked to grab my pencil box and leave all of the groups. I was then escorted down the long hallway, enclosed by brick walls, and into the special-education room. I stayed there until I was in fourth grade.

By fifth grade I picked up speed and began to excel in most of my coursework. My teachers liked to describe me as a "late bloomer," but I still saw myself as stupid. I would escape the insecurities I had with myself by picking up books and spending my days in the stories and with the characters on the pages. When I wasn't reading, I would go outside and play. Since I lived in the country, and away from my friends, I mostly played by myself. Being alone, I ended up creating several characters and scenes in my head that I would play out as I ran around the yard, climbed on the haystacks left over from when we had horses, or through the corridor of trees.

It was a treat when friends were allowed to come over and play with me. One of those treats happened as we were entering into our second week of our summer break. Megan had called to see if I'd like to go swimming with her. I usually didn't go to the public pool, since my dad had installed an inground pool in our backyard when I was an infant. Every time someone invited me to go swimming, I would try to get my parents to allow them to come over to our house, which would then ultimately lead to a sleepover party.

My parents both liked Megan, so they agreed to my request. The rest of the day we swam with my sister, and were both exhausted by the time it was dark outside. But I wanted to continue to play, so I constructed a makeshift tent in my bedroom by draping my blanket over my chairs and desk, and then placing encyclopedias on top of it all to hold everything in place. I stood up tall and puffed out my chest and pretended I was the hero who built the shelter on a lost island for a damsel in distress. Megan smiled and crawled under the blanket tent with me, but she wasn't impressed with the hard floor so she moved over to the bed. I wanted to move with her, but I was stubborn and too proud of my tent, so I stayed in place.

As her parents picked her up the next day, I yelled out, "See you at the softball game tomorrow!" We waved at each other and I watched her crawl into the back of her parents' minivan.

It was the last time I saw her.

That night I heard the distant sirens from an ambulance and wondered what was going on as I fell back to sleep, this time on my soft mattress. The next morning, when I headed out to the kitchen for breakfast, I noticed my parents' stiffened postures in the chairs around the table. My dad looked away from me and so I looked over toward my mom. I noticed her face was puffy. I watched as she wiped away her tears with a napkin.

"I just got off the phone, and, uh, Megan died last night in a car accident," she said.

I stopped breathing.

The seconds started to pass before I gasped for some air and let the tears stream down my face. My mind instantly started flipping through different scenarios, and I wanted all of those moments we had the day before to be part of a "Choose Your Own Adventure" book. I wanted to flip back the pages to the beginning and lead everyone on a different path after the wrong turn we had made before.

Over the next two days, guilt rushed over me. Each adventure I chose led to the same results. I clipped out the articles about the accident from the paper and laid them out on my bed. I kept looking at them, hoping the story would change, but it didn't.

I believed I was the cause of Megan's death. If I hadn't invited her over to my house and had her stay the night, then she and her parents wouldn't have gone when they did to check on their cows, I decided. If they would have gone at any other time, then they wouldn't have arrived at the intersection on that dusty gravel road right as another man drove through the stop sign. Their van wouldn't have been broadsided; and Megan wouldn't have flown out of the car, dying moments later. Superman might have been able to fly around the Earth's orbit and reverse time; I had to stay fixed to the ground and mourn. I never knew I could feel as much pain as I did about my body—my limitations—until her death.

I tried to repair things when we went to the visitation at her parents' house. Cars lined the gravel road that led up to their farmhouse. I watched as townspeople walked along the edge of the road, toward the two-story home, with their arms full of casserole dishes, breads, and pies.

When we stepped into the entryway, I lifted up a cream-colored envelope toward Megan's mom. I was worried her mom would look at me and scowl, but instead she reached her arms out and grabbed hold of me. She pulled me toward her and pressed my head against her stomach as one of her hands cupped the side of my cheek. She wouldn't let go, but squeezed me tighter as she sobbed. I stayed in her arms as the minutes passed. I wanted to cry with her, but I felt my energy being pulled into her. Staying strong for her was the least I could do.

Megan was the second friend I had lost due to a car accident.

After losing her, my sadness toward life shifted and traveled further into a dark depression. This included thoughts of suicide. My depression and desire to escape reality carried me to the pastures during the day, where I would venture to the farthest corner, but still be on our property.

My new escape required the use of a long stick to whack at the grass that stood taller than I did. My tears would start to fall when I arrived at a clearing where I had built a three-foot wall of intertwined sunflower stocks. I felt like the wall protected me from watching eyes. To protect me further, I stomped down a circular area in the grass and tucked myself inside the spot. I lay on my back to look up toward the clear sky, but my vision was blocked by the intermingling branches of the cedar trees, which ran a dividing line between our pasture and the fields full of cornstalks that stretched up to eight feet tall.

This was a secret spot, a spot that my sister and I named Fort Biscuit after our miniature schnauzer. I preferred being there alone. I couldn't cry in front of other people; I wanted to be seen as being tough, something I learned from watching my dad interact with my brother. Men don't cry. My desire to be a boy drove me, so I held back my tears until I was alone. I'd often cry myself to sleep in that spot, only to wake up to a tractor rolling down the gravel road adjacent to our little fort, or a distant whistle from the train tracks a half mile south from where I lay.

It was within the confines of my interwoven sunflower shelter that I vowed to give up my belief that I could turn into a boy. The magical powers I had hoped would listen to me never replied; my wishes fell onto deaf ears. These were the same ears that ignored my pleas to bring Megan back.

I lost all hope toward magical powers existing, with the exception of birthday wishes.

By my twelfth birthday I quit wishing to turn into a boy and started to wish that my body would just stop turning more female. With puberty I saw my breasts developing and my hips widening. The changes were taking away my androgynous build. The short brown hair that I had felt so proud of had now grown back out, hanging down near the middle of my back. My cheeks had rounded and my legs and stomach had become chubbier as my body was building up small amounts of fat stores in preparation for the growth spurts that I would experience over the next two years. At that time I didn't know that I would grow into the extra weight I had gained. I just knew that I felt uncomfortable and awkward from the changes; these feelings worsened and nearly crippled me when my menstrual cycle began. I was one of the last girls in my class to get her period. I knew this because I had watched the other girls write letters of congratulations on pieces of paper with a red-ink pen, before shoving the folded note into a locker. The locker would belong to the girl who had just joined the menstrual club, now a step closer to being a woman. I never received one of the letters because it was something I didn't want anyone to know. I just wanted it to stop.

My sister picked up on my insecurities and used them to her advantage. She would obnoxiously sing, "Fat and wide, fat and wide, you are very fat and wide" as she moved her hands out and up. I rarely put up a fight with her. I just watched as she skipped around me, singing the same verse over and over again. Her long, skinny legs would move up and down with each skip, causing her perfect ponytail to whip back and forth behind her like a horse swaying its tail.

I wanted to get back at my sister and prove to her that she was wrong. So as I blew out the candles on the homemade birthday cake, and looked up at everyone smiling and clapping, I decided I'd start focusing on making my body as fit as possible.

If I couldn't be a boy, at least I could make myself look like one. This idea came to me after watching women bodybuilders strain out different poses on television. I was fascinated by their prominent pectoral muscles, which engulfed their breasts, and their large bicep muscles, which popped out each time they flexed.

The next day I went down to our basement, where my dad was finishing his own workout. He stood next to the weight bench, arms leaning on top of the bench-press bar, while he caught his breath. His white T-shirt was drenched in sweat and his gray sweatpants were hiked up to his belly button. I laughed at our differences. I pulled my pants down as low as possible, while he pulled them up as high as he could.

"What do ya want?" he jokingly growled at me.

"I was wondering if you would teach me how to lift weights," I said.

"Sure," he responded, a smile formed on his face. "Let me just finish up and change shirts."

I sat down and watched him pull the long bar up to his chin before dropping it back down and repeating the motion. I was excited to start lifting, and to spend even more time with my dad. After he taught me some basic weight-lifting positions, I became hooked. From middle school to high school, I religiously lifted weights and jumped rope, along with playing golf and basketball with my school's sports teams. I didn't miss a day of working out. The only times I felt good were when sweat ran down my face and drenched my shirts. I couldn't stop; I believed that if I did stop, my body would lose its athletic edge and I would then be swallowed up by all of the bad feelings that followed me every day. Even with all of the activities I was involved in, I felt disheartened when I looked at my reflection and knew it didn't come close to resembling the women, who were built like men, that I had seen on TV.

During my sophomore year of high school, I sat in a physical education class and listened to my teacher talk about portion sizes. It was then that I realized working out wasn't enough. I needed to watch what I ate, too. I decided I would ask my mom for help with my diet after the school bus dropped me off that day. I entered our house through our garage; and when I smelled freshly baked cupcakes sitting in the kitchen, I immediately knew a diet would be challenging. My mom was standing over them, whipping around thick and creamy vanilla frosting. I watched as she spread the frosting over the top of the chocolate chip cupcakes, one of my favorites.

"Hey, Mom," I said as I set my backpack down on the kitchen table.

"Hi," she said. She dipped the knife back into the metal bowl full of frosting. "How was your day?"

"Okay. . . ." I looked at the cupcakes; my mouth started to salivate. "Mom . . . can you help me lose weight?"

"Lose weight?" she asked in disbelief. "Kim, you don't have to lose weight. You just simply have to eat right."

"How do I do that?" I asked.

"Here. . . ." She dropped the knife into the bowl and went over to her recipe box. She pulled out a fresh index card and started to neatly write something I couldn't see; her hand blocked the words she was printing. "Take this and put it up on your bulletin board. It will help you." I peered over her hand and saw a "Column A" and a "Column B" written on the top of the card. I looked closer and could read the first three foods listed in each column. "A" had Jell-O, apples, and lean meats; "B" listed buttered popcorn, bagels, and candy. Before handing me the card, she wrote "Good Foods" and "Bad Foods" above the two columns. I took the index card and taped it to the full-size mirror that hung on the back of my bedroom door. I then hung a collage, which I had made in art class, on the wall next to the door; it showed different sports icons, weight-lifting positions, and hard bodies.

I began to look at my collage and index card to gain motivation before heading down to our basement to do a workout, if I didn't feel like I had enough during the day at school. My favorite workout video was one where Jane Fonda danced around in a leotard. My dad called her "Janey Baby"; so when I went through the hour-long aerobic video, I found myself yelling at her, "Come on, Janey Baby, make me feel it burn!" The aches I felt in my abdominal muscles and my butt would help with my anxiety as I finished up the tape, along with all of the clapping people on the TV who were dancing in place for a cooldown.

After turning off the TV, I would retreat to the confines of my room, where time would pass by without me noticing. I was always too focused on studying my body and how it was changing with each layer of clothes I stripped off. The first article of clothing to come off was always my baseball cap. I wore it to keep my hair out of my face while I worked out. After being freed from the hat, I would watch as my hair dropped down to my shoulders. The long, sweaty strands of hair made me yearn for a haircut like I had when I was younger, but I felt short hair would draw too much attention to me at school. I was tired of being teased and wanted to fit in, so I had grown my hair out and would attempt to style it like all the other girls.

My hair disappeared from my sight as I pulled off my cutoff T-shirt and threw it toward my plastic hamper. I looked at my breasts; they were pressed down and confined by a blue sports bra. I would only wear sports bras, the other bras felt too feminine, too revealing. My stomach was flat and I could make out ridges to my abs. I knew I also had to strip off my shorts, but I couldn't bring myself to do it. The parts of my body that scared me the most were my thighs and butt. Instead of stripping completely down, I was able to lift up on the red-mesh fabric to expose my right thigh. My quadriceps bulged and curved under my skin. From the results I was seeing, I knew I had to keep pushing myself during my workouts.

My classmates noticed my increased muscularity and used it to make fun of me. Rumors started to cycle through the halls that I was a lesbian, even though I had a boyfriend. This label horrified me. I had kissed girls during slumber parties, but the reason they chose me was because I was like a boy. I knew two girls together weren't accepted in my community, and definitely not accepted by my parents.

This was made clear when I had mentioned to my mom that I was thinking about becoming a physical education teacher when I went to college. She looked at me and scoffed, "PE teachers have the reputation of being lesbians." Her statement surprised me. I rarely heard the term used, and was stunned she even knew what it was.

My dad seemed proud of my more masculine behaviors and appearance when I was on the basketball court pushing around the opponents, or out in the yard helping him plant trees or build new stands to set old farm supplies from his parents' homestead upon. He didn't seem as proud when it was time for me to fit into the female social roles at school or community events.

When I was in high school, the most tension I had with my parents revolved around the clothes I wanted to wear, and whether or not I had a boyfriend. My brother's innocent joke during a visit home from college didn't help my parents' insecurities with how I presented myself. After church on that Sunday, we all went to my grandma's house for dinner. I had made sure to toss a bag into the car that contained a change of clothes for after the church sermon.

When we arrived at my grandma's house, I didn't waste any time running toward her spare bedroom and changing out of the dress clothes I had been forced to wear. I was a huge Chicago Bulls fan and had just bought a jersey with Dennis Rodman's number on it. I quickly changed into a T-shirt and pulled my jersey over it. I felt a wave of peace wash over me after being freed from the blouse, constricting tights, and a hideous floral skirt.

I opened the door to the bedroom and started walking out to join my family, when I heard my brother's voice: "Hey, if you want to be like Dennis Rodman, you're gonna have to start wearing women's clothing."

My sister laughed. She hated the way that I dressed and often referred to me as "Tim, my little brother."

"Thanks, Greg," I said before leaving the room and going outside to retreat further inside myself.

Within a week my parents jumped on Greg's bandwagon.

"Those pants make you look like you have an old man's butt," my dad said out of the blue.

I was passing through the family room toward my bedroom after school, but I was stopped short by his comment. I turned around, scared to make eye contact with him. He was sitting in his recliner, still in his work clothes, which consisted of dark brown slacks and a short-sleeved, button-up white shirt. He held the town's newspaper in his hands, but he had it folded down to look at me.

"What?" I asked.

"Why do you always wear jeans that are too big for you? The backside is hanging down so far, Kim, you don't even look like you have a butt."

"Sorry," I said before turning back around and escaping to my room. I had hoped the discussion would be dropped because later that day he asked me if I wanted to go out to a hamburger joint with him and Mom. We didn't eat out very often, so I saw this as being a treat. This was short lived. As we sat at the table and waited for our burgers, my dad started in on me again.

"Don't you want to feel pretty?" he asked.

The word "pretty" made me cringe. I started to push around the crackers I had crumbled over my salad.

"You'd be pretty like your mom and sister if you just wore some makeup and maybe put a little effort into the clothes you wear."

I looked away from him and over at my mom. I had hoped she would defend me, but I knew she was thinking the same thing.

"You wouldn't have to wear a lot of makeup, just a little. . . . That's all I like to wear," she suggested, trying to defuse my embarrassment.

I felt like they wanted me to go out to dinner so they could trap me in a place where I had nowhere to escape. In reality, my parents liked to set the stage to talk about what was on their minds and give suggestions for ways to improve things they viewed as potential problems. There were a lot of times when I found their rational approaches to be helpful. However, I could never tell them that when it came to things about me that made them uncomfortable, their perceived fixes just made me hurt more.

All I wanted was to feel loved and supported.

Their rational comments continued until I was saved by the waitress, who slapped down our plates full of hot curly fries and hamburgers the size of our heads. We all turned our attention to our dinner, but sadly it was only a temporary distraction.

The next day my mom grabbed me for a surprise trip into town. I knew we weren't going to the sports store when she parked our car in front of a large brick home. It belonged to one of my teachers, who was also the head football coach. I had a brief moment when I thought my parents suddenly had a change of heart and were going to let me try out for the football team. That moment passed, though, when I realized I was there to see his wife, a Mary Kay makeup saleswoman. I could have thrown a tantrum when we walked into the house, but I wanted to get it over with so

I could go home and play basketball in our driveway.

"That's right! You're a natural," the wife said as she watched me put the makeup on. She was proud to see I had picked up on the proper techniques that she had just demonstrated, but I felt like her nice comments came from a place of feeling sorry for me.

My mouth was wide open and my hands shook as I pressed the black pencil against my skin and ran it around my upper eyelid. When I was finished, I looked at my reflection in the mirror. My eyelids had three tones smudged together—white, green, and brown. My lips were more accentuated with a light pink lipstick, and my cheeks looked like I had just finished a long run due to the brushes of blush I had swiped across my cheekbones.

I felt like a clown.

My mom and the wife kept commenting on how good I looked, and how I would turn heads at the school's dance that was coming up.

I watched as my mom handed over some money and was then handed a green bag, which contained the products I had running across my face.

When we got home, I ran to the bathroom to wash off the makeup and then placed the bag in a clothes drawer, where it stayed most days. I broke down and smeared the colors on my face when my family's disapproving looks made me want to hide.

By my senior year, I was scrambling like the other kids in my class to find the identity that would define me outside of my school and rural community. Even with my social anxiety, I was involved in a myriad of clubs and sports. These kept me active and gave me something to focus on outside myself. Pictures of me made frequent appearances in the town's newspaper, the *Aurora Register.* Drama, speech, honor band, foreign language club, honor society, basketball, golf, government day—the list continued. I was known as a "Goody Two-shoes." Yet, I did occasionally "break the rules." Here and there I would sneak a swig of rum from my dad's bar, or go out with friends to unapproved places.

One brisk winter night, boredom got the better of my friends, and we decided to head to the city next to ours for a Saturday evening on the town. I was told by my parents not to go to Grand Island at night. However, at age seventeen and nearing graduation, I had small moments of rebellion against my parents' wishes. We all piled into a white Buick and sped down the highway. Being the person who gets motion sick in the backseat, I chose the front-passenger seat and became the music bitch, the one who flipped through the radio stations until we hit a station that made our heads snap back and forth. When the beats started, I would reach for the speaker adjustments and turn the bass knob all the way to the right as I turned the treble all the way to the left.

We had no particular destination in mind. We were free spirits cruising down the road and open to whatever events led us to excitement. I wasn't good at being a free spirit; so internally I was freaking out and could feel my anxiety increasing the blood pressure in my chest. My anxiety turned to a lump in my throat as my friend flipped up the car's blinker and made a turn to the right, off the highway and onto "the strip." This was a mile-long stretch of road that was laden with stoplights, convenience stores, and fast-food chains. The city had posted signs stating that cruising was illegal, but the businesses that lined each side attracted teenagers like ants traveling along a picnic blanket scattered with the remnants of a meal.

At each red light, we crept to a stop and rolled our windows down so we could scope out the occupants of the cars that pulled up next to us. If there were guys in the car, we would start talking to them. If there were girls, we would poke fun. The word "bitch" was a common reference shouted on the strip. I was the quiet one whenever we pulled up to other cars. I was scared of guys being turned off if they saw me, and intimidated by girls making fun of my big nose and wild, curly hair.

While my friends all turned to look out the passenger-side windows, I remained facing forward, but I used my periphery vision to peek over toward our stoplight neighbors. This time it was a blue Pontiac Grand Am, with gray plastic trim. A whiff of cigarette smoke mixed with burned oil hit my nostrils. Two girls, with long fingernails and long blond hair, looked over at us. One was chewing gum; the other started to point our way.

"Come on, you want a piece of me, bitch!" one of my friends obnoxiously yelled while leaning out the window in the back. The girl chewing the gum started yelling back at us when the light turned green. We slammed on the accelerator of the car; tires squealed, along with my car mate's laughter; the girl's voice faded into the wind..

The next day, I knew my identity after graduation would not be being a rebel because guilt immediately started to choke me as I drove up the driveway toward my house. I was scared of my parents finding out where I had gone and became paranoid. So after entering the house, I immediately tossed my clothes into the washer to get rid of potential evidence, the smell of cigarette smoke. I felt better after I had successfully moved the clothes from the washer to the dryer.

As everything began to tumble, I snuck through the house toward my bedroom. I liked to sit in my room and listen to music as I drew pictures or worked on my homework. That day I was frustrated with how abnormal I felt the night before. So instead of listening to some alternative rock, I popped in soft-core rap. I found that the music-driven emotions rushing through me allowed me to feel centered—the downside to this was it often led me to crying.

Whenever I had crying spells, I didn't want to leave until the puffiness under my eyes and redness around my nose diminished, but I couldn't allow myself to do that if I had laundry finished in the dryer. I liked to grab them when they were still warm so that I could get things hung up before they wrinkled. If there was one thing I hated more than doing laundry, it was ironing out the wrinkles. My adulthood OCD trumped my crying; I knew I had to pick myself up off the blue shag carpet and leave the walls that confined my teenage angst. Before leaving, I wiped away my tears, straightened my back, and took in a deep breath. I then swung open my door and faced the dark and empty hallway. Now whatever emotions I had just experienced didn't exist.

I slowly tiptoed through the hallway and into the living room, which sat adjacent to where my dad was watching TV. I was hoping he wouldn't see my shadow or hear me move through the house. I made it to the laundry room successfully. But as I was pulling the clothes out of the dryer, I looked over my shoulder and saw him standing beside me.

"What's wrong with you tonight?" he asked.

"Nothing . . ." I turned to leave, afraid of him making eye contact and seeing my puffy face.

"I don't want you listening to that crap," he said, referring to my rap music. His stern voice stopped me in my tracks; the warm laundry was clasped in my arms. "That music is making you a negative person."

I was scared if I said anything, he would follow me into my room and swipe all of my music that he didn't approve of; so I quickly looked at him, looked away, and then retreated to my bedroom.

His words repeated in my head the next day as I threw myself onto a green seat confined within a school bus. I was joined by other girls piling onto the bus; we were all part of the basketball team and were traveling out of town to play the last game of the season.

Not only was it the last game of the season, it was also the last game I would play with the Aurora Huskies. I tried to shake my emotions by talking with others on the bus, but felt heavy as we arrived and entered the locker room. I pulled on my jersey and looked in the mirror. On the red jersey there was a large number 40. It had been my number for the last three years, but after that night it would be passed on to one of the incoming sophomores. My frustration from the night before turned into numbness as we walked onto the basketball court.

I played horribly that night.

I wanted to be known as a great basketball player, but that night I didn't even take a shot at the basket.

At the end of the game, the buzzer sounded, leaving our team, the Lady Huskies, with another disappointing loss. Before exiting the court, we all walked in a single-file line with our hands up to give our opponents high fives and congratulate them on their win. While each sweaty palm brushed against mine, I tried to avoid looking up into the bleachers and seeing my parents. I had to, though, because it would be the last time I would have them looking down at me and seeing me as something other than their daughter.

It was my last time being player number 40.

On my high-school graduation day, I vowed that I would go to college and accomplish two things to cement an identity that all of us approved of for me. The first goal I had was not to gain weight. All of the girls who gained weight were made fun of when they returned to our hometown for visits. The second was to find a boyfriend who would want to marry me. Most people from my hometown were engaged by the time their freshman year of college ended. I knew that I could squash the rumors surrounding me about being a lesbian—and make my parents proud—if I also joined the fiancée club.

After a few weeks in college, I began to wonder if I would be able to reach either of my goals. The embarrassment I felt on account of my body, and the fight I had against my biology, affected my development as a person, especially within romantic relationships.

I had had boyfriends throughout high school and knew I was initially attracted to them, but I kept them around because I liked having a male companion to play sports and joke around with. Inevitably they became my best friends. For them, the longer we were together, the further they would take the intimacy between us. The increase in touching and exploring of our bodies made me feel more anxious and emotionally distressed. I began to experience different sensations when I was in a dark room with them: a part of me wanted to explore our bodies, and the other part wanted to hide or disappear. I was scared. I tried to figure out why I felt so uncomfortable, and decided it was because of my body and my looks. Even though my body in high school resembled that of a swimmer—a v-shaped torso, broad shoulders, and defined muscles—I believed I was fatter than all the other girls and that my facial features, including my large nose, round cheeks, and freckles, were unattractive. In college I gave myself one more chance to push past my insecurities, and I put that plan into action on the day I took a risk and talked to a guy I saw on my college campus.

The trees were dropping the leaves that had finished changing colors for the season in preparation for Nebraska's cold winters. I was walking toward Bessey Hall on the University of Nebraska's campus, which was where most of my classes in anthropology were housed. I had chosen anthropology and English as my undergraduate majors because cultures were something that fascinated me, and escaping into books was what had kept me alive.

Out of the corner of my eye, I felt like I caught a glimpse of someone I knew. As I looked closer, I saw a gawky guy, with a prominent nose, snacking on a peanut butter and jelly sandwich.

"Chris?" I asked.

He looked up from his sandwich and book; our matching green eyes made contact. He hesitated a moment before saying, "Oh, hey, Kim." A large smile grew on his face, exposing his straight teeth.

I knew Chris from my hometown. He was four years older than I was, but we had played in jazz band together during the school year. When he was in college, he would organize a summer jazz band that met in the attic of a dilapidated antiques store located on our town square. It was always hot up there, so we would open the windows, which faced the town's brick-and-mortar courthouse, to let a breeze flow through. Along with the breeze, the sweet smells of freshly baked dough, warm tomato sauce, and baked cheese would waft through the windows from the pizza shop next door.

I had had a crush on him then. We both loved to play jazz and were serious about practicing. I watched as he blew out improv on his trombone, and then I came back at him with my fingers running over my saxophone. We had a lot in common, but I never told him about my crush. Our ages were too far apart to be anything more than friends.

"Wow, I haven't seen you in ages. How are you doing?" I asked. I was slightly amazed at how social I was being. Usually, when I saw people I knew, I would duck my head down and try to avoid eye contact because I was afraid they wouldn't want to talk with me.

"Good, good. I'm just reading about bison before class." He tapped his open book.

I looked down and saw a sketch of a fossilized bone with notations about size and formation. I felt a warm sensation rush into my stomach when I realized we were both in the anthropology program. He was studying archaeology and I was specializing in cultural.

"Hey, cool. . . . We're studying the same major."

"We are?" he asked. I noticed he seemed happily surprised by another thing that we had in common. It was also nice to see that he was still in college; his time in the National Guard and interests in music had delayed his studies in college.

"Uh, we should go out sometime for coffee or a Coke," I said. I took this line from my dad, who suggested I try it as a way to get to know someone. I hadn't had the chance to use it until now.

"That would be nice. How about you give me your phone number and e-mail address." He extended his notebook toward me and held out a pen.

I jotted down my information. The letters were slightly jagged due to my nerves. I wasn't sure he would call me, but the next day there was a message on my voice mail.

As we began to date, I felt more uncomfortable in my skin.

This discomfort started to hit its boiling point in the spring when I had to be the maid of honor at my sister's wedding. I was terrified by the idea of wearing a dress. When I moved away to college, I left behind the dresses that my mom had bought me over the years. I preferred my corduroy pants, leather work boots, and button-up shirts. My body had been hidden, up until the evening of the rehearsal dinner.

I had put on the outfit that my mom had picked out and had left hanging on the outside of my closet, before I broke down crying.

"What's wrong?" my mom asked. She was standing in a blouse and slip, only halfway dressed for the evening.

"I hate dresses, Mom. Everything feels uncomfortable. I don't want to wear them. . . . Can't I wear these pants?" I held up a pair of black pin-striped pants, which were held up by a drawstring.

"No, that isn't formal enough." She grabbed the pants from me and hung them back up in my closet.

My sister rolled her eyes, tired of having to deal with my breakdowns every time I was forced to wear dresses or other feminine clothing. The scene that was playing out had happened many times before as if my sister and I were five years old again. It was a scene that only involved the women in the Sallans household. I knew that my dad wouldn't tolerate my tantrums.

We settled on a floor-length skirt and cream-colored top, covered by a sweater vest. I kept my leather jacket on most of the night. It covered my top and the shape of my butt in the dress. I knew, however, that the next day at the wedding, there was no way I could hide under a jacket.

Anxiety shot through my body as I looked at myself in the dress that my mom had made for the wedding. Cream fabric ran around the top of the dress by my shoulders and breasts to complement the shimmering maroon material that circled my hips and went down past my knees. I didn't want to hurt my mom's feelings, but I hated the dress and how it stretched across my breasts, hips, and stomach. I wouldn't be happy in any dress, but this one brought out even more of my insecurities. I tried to hide how I felt; I knew the day was about my sister, and not about me.

My anxiousness got the better of me as I walked down the aisle, on the drab yellow carpet that had been in the church since the 1970s. I was paranoid that everyone watching me was looking at my butt. I tried to push out my insecurities by concentrating on putting my left foot before my right foot, following the beats from the organ playing at the front of the church. I wanted to do the walk right and proper, like all women should do, but I couldn't. I walked fast and with a limp, a habit that I acquired from my days as an athlete in high school.

I took my place at the front of the church and cinched my butt as I sucked my stomach in as far as it would go. I stayed that way throughout the ceremony, fighting the voices screaming in my head about how I looked and what the people sitting in the pews were thinking of me. While standing there, in front of everyone, I made a pact to try and change my shape again. I had to do something to be more feminine and beautiful, because I couldn't continue living a life where I felt like I didn't fit in. To try and help my distress, after the ceremony, I quickly stripped out of the dress and put on my baggy jeans and T-shirt, before heading to the reception.

When I arrived, I went to every table and found the stranded bottles of champagne. I lifted each bottle and shook it. If there was alcohol left inside, I raised it to my lips and downed the remaining content, hoping it would ease my nerves.

Relieved to have the wedding over, I shifted my focus back to my schoolwork.

I had only five weeks left before I'd have one year of college under my belt. I knew the passing of my first year would be when Chris would graduate from his program. We both didn't know what that would mean for us. We didn't really even know what our relationship meant. We had been dating, on and off, for eight months, but we weren't serious. When we went out, we would have dinner and then chat, or go to his place and eat pasta while drinking beer. Our intimacy was mostly limited to kissing and holding each other. We tried to do more, but we weren't very compatible, and both of us were scared to get too close.

Even though we weren't in love, a part of me liked the idea of marrying Chris. I knew he didn't have the same idea, partly because of my age and also because his parents felt I wasn't the right person for him. To try and explore how our lives could intertwine, we planned a camping trip after his graduation. It was supposed to be a celebration and a chance to take some great photos of windmills retired from their years of service and prairie dogs claiming the ground as their territory.

I learned very quickly that nights are cold in the Sandhills of Nebraska. As I was packing, I hadn't thought about the sand's inability to absorb heat as the sun tucks away for the night and the moon moves up in the sky, allowing the sweltering heat from the day to take a break.

We didn't bring a tent, but instead just tossed our sleeping bags out over the sand next to the fire that was slowly starting to die out. Chris's long and lanky body lay next to me. His arms were placed behind his head as we both looked up toward the sky.

I felt cold, not just because of the temperature, but because of the chemistry between us. The crackling of the dying fire kept us company and filled the awkward silence.

We had originally planned to hike another day and spend another night; but during our second day out in the hills, Chris decided we should drive the five hours back home. We gathered up our camping gear and tossed it into his little silver pickup truck. I had never felt lonelier in my life than I did with him as we wound through the back roads of Nebraska, passing barren land, witnessing cows eating the small scraps of grass they could find, and seeing towns composed of two buildings and a saloon.

We listened to Dar Williams's cassette tapes and didn't say much. I knew from the energy in the truck that I had done something wrong. Every relationship I had been in, I always felt that I was defective, unacceptable, and unattractive.

Relief filled me when he turned onto the gravel driveway that led up to my house. As I stepped out of his truck, I pulled the back of my shirt away from my sweaty skin. He hadn't run the air-conditioning the whole trip, which had just added to the uneasiness.

"Will I talk with you later?" I asked.

He ran his right hand through the waves of his brown hair as he gripped his steering wheel with his left.

"Not tonight. I'm going to go play pool with my dad," he said.

I noticed his voice was higher in pitch. I didn't want to accept the possibility of him telling me a lie. I watched as he backed his truck up, the sound of its engine revved with urgency as he shifted into first gear.

That good-bye was our last. I had been dumped like the clothes worth forgetting at the Laundromat.

After a few days had passed, I knew he wasn't going to call me, not even to give me some closure in the relationship. From the way he treated me, and from the way I felt with him romantically, I decided it was time for me to change, but I didn't really know how I would do it.

Whenever I felt sad or uncomfortable, I would turn my attention toward my body. My hands ran over my stomach and down over my thighs. I began to mourn the loss of my firm oblique muscles and flat stomach, which over the course of my freshman year had started to retain more water and form more curves. I still maintained that the changes in my shape were due to the "freshman fifteen," the age-old myth that suggests women gain fifteen pounds their freshman year of college.

I didn't understand that as a woman ages, her hips expand and her breasts become fuller. This is biology's way of preparing her for childbearing. Mine didn't have the common courtesy of asking me if I wanted this to happen. It just assumed that all estrogen-based bodies are seeking this change. I labeled myself as fat, and decided I needed to change to be seen as more feminine.

For me, at age eighteen, my view of feminine was skinny. This led me to believe that if I wanted to be accepted by my parents and potential mates, I needed to appear more like a woman. I needed to be more feminine. To accomplish this, I decided that I needed to be skinny.

A week after the awkward breakup, I was sprawled out on my dad's recliner, watching TV with my mom. Bored from surfing channels, I stopped on a teaser for what would be featured on *60 Minutes* that night. The announcer enthusiastically closed with, "Learn how to lose fat and look great with this new diet that doctors love, the Sugar Busters diet."

My disinterest in *60 Minutes* quickly shifted to curiosity as I listened to a roundtable of three doctors talk about the premise of the diet. I soaked up their bullet points, which were to eat very small, if any, amounts of carbohydrates and sugar; this included not eating carrots, apples, peas, and oranges. I was a little confused by how one could lose weight by not eating certain fruits and vegetables, but that night I decided I'd begin on the diet and see if it would work.

I was a skeptic at first. I had grown up with the belief that I was fat, even though my grandma always said I was just "big boned." If what she said was true, then I knew a diet wouldn't change my bone structure.

The strong smell of latex paint and a mixture of bleach hit my nostrils as the door swung open to the single dorm room I would be residing in during my sophomore year of college. I was wearing a black tank top to show off my tan, which I had acquired from working the summer on a road construction crew. I also wore a pair of jean shorts that were five sizes too big for me. I kept pulling them up as I was carrying boxes up to my room. My waistline had gotten smaller over the summer. The diet I had started was finally starting to work. I was happy with the weight I had lost and was starting to see muscle tone again.

After setting up my room, I went across campus to visit the friends whom I had made the prior year.

"Kim, have you lost some weight?" one of girls asked. She had just gotten off the elevator with her parents, who were struggling with her dorm fridge.

"Yeah . . . thanks for noticing!" It felt good to hear a positive comment, and it motivated me to stay on my new routine.

"We are all thinking of going out tonight. Do you want to join us?" she asked.

"Sure." I was surprised I had said yes, but my new appearance made me want to be seen by people.

I took a break from my diet that night and decided to drink alcohol with everyone. Every can of Busch Light that was handed to me, I accepted and gulped down. The beer ran down my throat like water, and I started to experience a tingly feeling down my spine, which relaxed every muscle in my body. We started out at a house party, but ended up at a guy's town house near the university. None of us knew who he was, but he had a nice place, good music, and more beer. We stayed.

For fun we all decided to practice our golf swings with Wiffle balls in his yard. I was amazed at how good my swing was when I was drunk. I hit several balls, one of which hooked right, so I decided to venture out and find it. I heard a car pull up behind me while I was wandering the streets.

"Damn, girl. Do you work out?" a guy asked while leaning outside the passenger window of a silver-blue Monte Carlo. There were four other guys in the car, but I couldn't see their faces. All I could make out was their heads bobbing to the bass of the music and their ball caps sitting sideways on their heads.

"Yeah, I guess you could say so." I stood up a little taller and looked down at my short-cropped gray tank top and khaki slacks. I filled them out, but it was a nice shape.

"Well, you look really good." He looked me up and down before licking his lips.

I was drunk, but I knew he was trying to pick me up, so I acted fast.

"Thanks, but I have to go. I lost my ball," I said. I spun around and swayed back toward the party.

The guy who owned the house started dancing with me in the living room, and then grabbing me and then making out with me. I kissed him back. It was the first time I had kissed a black man, and I loved the fullness and smoothness of his lips. I then felt his hand go down the front of my pants and I felt the urge to stay the night with him. I wanted to be bad, and I wanted to know if I could really sleep with a man.

My friends, concerned about my ability to make good judgments, dragged me off the stairs, where we were making out, and out of the house. They pushed me into the backseat of the car and I was able to wave at the guy before I passed out. I ended up going back to their dorm room and crashing on the bottom bunk, too drunk to go any farther.

Before I fell asleep, I did two hundred crunches and vowed that I wouldn't drink again. I was afraid of the calories, and also my actions with men when I drank.

Over the course of the next six months, my face sank in and my complexion turned to a pasty yellow-gray, making me look like I had jaundice or hepatitis.

The beginning of my second semester, I started to suspect that there was something wrong with me when I began an essay on eating disorders. All of the symptoms and descriptions of hunger pains were happening to me. Before now, I had ignored my body's hunger signals, and I had brushed off the whispered comments from friends on how much weight I had lost.

I hadn't considered getting help until I visited with my parents after they had returned home from a winter vacation in Texas. When I ran into the house to give my mom a hug, all I saw was my dad standing in the doorway with a look of fearful disgust on his face.

To their eyes I had transformed into a stranger.

"You're so thin," he said as he wrapped his hand around my twig arm. Just four months ago my arms were well formed, with muscle and strength.

The hat I had pulled down over my eyes was lifted from my head by his hand. My brittle hair fell in front of my eyes, covering my pasty complexion. I was uncomfortable and ashamed as I felt my parents' inspecting eyes looking over me and judging me.

"You don't even look like yourself," he said.

As I drove down that day, I kept thinking about how they would react when they saw me. Now my own father barely recognized me.

"Where is my Kimberly?" he asked.

I honestly couldn't give him an answer. I was confused.

"I'm right here, Mom . . . Dad. . . ?"

They didn't reply.

Later that night, while we were watching *The Tonight Show with Jay Leno,* I decided to ask my dad his professional opinion about a bump I had noticed under my breastbone. I was scared that it was cancer and didn't know what to do.

"Dad, what is this lump right here?" I asked as I reluctantly pulled up the front of my T-shirt and set his hand on it.

"God, Kim. That's your xiphoid process, a bone underneath your sternum. You've gotten so damn skinny, it is sticking out!" He took his hand away. "What the hell did you do while we were away?"

I blamed the change in my weight on the cafeteria food. My parents nodded their heads and advised me to eat more protein. They kept reassuring me that during the summer, when I was home to work with the road construction crew again, they would fix meals that would get me back to health.

I wanted to be healthy, too. So when I returned to campus, I scheduled an appointment for a yearly exam at the health center. I knew I hadn't had a menstrual cycle in over five months, so I decided I should receive a professional opinion. I was nervous when the health center called and asked me to come back in to review my lab work.

When I had gone in for the yearly exam, I didn't know my blood would be drawn, so I had eaten breakfast that morning instead of fasting. I felt embarrassed as I sat on the exam table, for the second time in a week. The paper underneath my butt kept making noises as I shifted my position in an attempt to get comfortable. I heard a light knock on the door before the doctor opened it and slowly made her way in. She had my chart in her hands and was flipping between the two-page lab report.

She smiled at me and said, "Hi, Kim, how are you today?"

"Fine," I said.

"We called you back because I am a bit concerned with some of the numbers that came back on your labs."

"Okay."

"So the one that concerns me the most is your blood glucose—"

"I'm sorry," I interrupted her to confess. "I had breakfast that morning. I didn't know I was supposed to fast."

"You had breakfast?" she asked with concern in her voice. "What did you have?"

"Just some Cheerios and a banana," I said. "Oh, and some coffee."

"Well, that concerns me even more." She looked down at my chart and scratched her head.

"It does?"

"Yes. Your blood glucose level is at thirty-three milligrams."

"Okay."

"The normal range is between seventy to one hundred twenty-five." She stood there for a moment and looked at me. She then looked at my chart and noted my height and weight. "Do you have any classes this morning?"

"No, I'm done for today," I said, confused by her question.

"Just a second, I'll be right back." I watched as she left the exam room. I sat there for another five more minutes before she returned with a business card in her hand. "I've made you an appointment in an hour to see this therapist. I feel like you would benefit from visiting with her." She handed me the card. I looked at it and then back toward her. "I want you to come back in a few weeks."

"Okay," I said. I thought about skipping the appointment. I didn't want someone to fix me. I didn't want to be big again, but I went for the first session and then returned for a second session. On some level I knew I needed help.

Soft sounds of birds chirping and water rushing through a stream filtered through the speakers of a CD player, which sat in the corner of her office. I felt confined, exposed, and vulnerable as I sat on the blue couch. She was positioned directly across from me, legal notepad in her lap, legs crossed.

She had chin-length sandy-blond hair, which she pushed behind her small ears. Her features were small, just like her height, and I assumed she was a gymnast forty years ago when she was a teenager. She had a small gold chain attached to her glasses, which she kept perched on the tip of her nose.

"You stopped shaking your foot," she said, gesturing toward my leg before squinting in preparation for my reaction. It was only our second session and she had already picked up on the little things I did when anxious.

I glanced down at my Nike tennis shoe set on top of my left knee. "Yeah, I guess I did."

"Maybe you don't feel as edgy today."

"Yeah, maybe I don't . . . I guess."

I didn't tell her that I had just finished running six miles and lifting weights for an hour; my body was exhausted.

"I checked over the questionnaires you returned to me." She reached for a yellow portfolio envelope marked *Kimberly Sallans.*

"What did it say?" I asked.

"Well, Kim. What has me concerned the most right now is your self-esteem." She showed me a bar graph. "If you look here, most women are in this area of the chart." The graphite of her pencil marked a line midway through the paper. "And here is where you ranked." Her pencil led me all the way to the top. "You are basically off the charts, meaning you don't hold yourself in very high regard." We sat there for a moment in silence. "Do you have anything you would like to add?"

"No, that pretty much hit the nail on the head." I leaned back on the couch. I could have told her that my self-esteem was at the bottom of the totem pole without wasting my time filling out the questionnaire.

I left the therapy session and headed to Andrews Hall for my English class. My Hanes T-shirt and khaki cargo pants hung on my frame. My thin arms hung to my sides as I slid my feet over the linoleum-lined floors.

"There's 'Skinny,'" I heard a guy whisper to another.

A smile came across my face as I reached my hand up to my stomach and rubbed the muscles that went in and out with my short breaths. The heroin look was what I wanted.

I wanted to resemble a model whom all the other girls would look at and think, *She's tough. Look at how her clothes just hang on her body. She must have excellent willpower.*

I didn't see what other people saw. I only heard the comments hitting me as I passed by them in the hallways, cafeteria, or on the streets.

"Jesus, that girl is sick! She looks disgusting."

"Someone give her a hamburger."

I had one more session with my therapist before I returned home for the summer. She sat across from me, waiting for me to talk. The silence hung between us before she took a breath in and said, "To tell you the truth, Kim, I'm concerned. . . . Summer is here now. You're moving back home and we won't be there."

To hear her say "we" made me feel uncomfortable. The image of a whole eating-disorder team working on my file was strange.

"I don't think there is any reason to worry. I will be back with my parents. I'll have good food and I can start playing sports with people again." I thought I was cured of the disorder at this point, but unfortunately I was just beginning.

"Well, if you need anything, there is someone in Grand Island you can talk to. Let me give you her number."

I stopped her before she could get a Post-it note.

"I'll be fine, really."

After the session I walked back to my dorm, where my dad was waiting by the door to help me move back home. In my hands I held a book, *The Perfection Trap: A Book for Young Women with Eating Disorders.*

"Well, what did she say?" he asked, even though he already knew the answer.

Tears started to cover my eyes, making my vision blurry. "I have a problem, Dad."

"Well, duh, Kim. I could have told you that. Just wait, though. When you get home, you'll have good meat and other foods to eat."

He thought it was all because of food; most people do. After I got home, I quickly realized that I should have taken that phone number from my therapist because the summer wasn't fine, and the food only made things worse.

"Kim, we're going into town." My dad's voice was muffled by the closed door between us.

"Okay" was my only response as I lay on the floor counting with my sit-ups and crunches. I waited until I heard his footsteps move away from my bedroom door and then waited for the slam of the door leading into our garage.

When I didn't hear anything else rustling in the house, I ran out to the living room and stared out the front window. I watched as their blue Buick Park Avenue pulled out of our long gravel driveway and turned left toward town. My heart skipped a beat. I was alone and my stomach needed something. I ran into my room and grabbed a hard pack of Camels out of my camera case, a perfect hiding spot.

My hands shook as I fumbled with the cellophane, which wrapped around the box. The bitter aroma of nicotine hit my nostrils as I pulled back the gold foil and placed my fingers on one of the round tips.

Knowing I couldn't smoke inside, I walked to the back of the house, opened the sliding door and stood on our porch. I stared at the trees that were lined up in a long row in the backyard and listened to the blackbirds caw as the smoke rose around me. The tension in my body left as I held the cancer stick between my fingers and knelt down into a catcher's squat. I watched myself in the glass of our sliding door. I watched how I inhaled the smoke and then blew circle O's out.

Every moment that passed, I felt closer to being like Karen Carpenter, my anorexic role model. I wanted to be skinny like her—and at the point I was at, die like her. I smoked until I heard my dog start to growl; a car was coming.

Fuck, they're back, I thought as I stubbed out my snack and threw the evidence under the wood-planked porch.

"What have you been doing?" they asked when they walked into the house with sacks of groceries in their arms.

"Nothing, like usual," I quietly mumbled as I walked past them and back to my bedroom.

I went to work the next day, only to be stuck outside in a downpour of rain while pulling noxious weeds from our interstate's medians. When I got back home, I felt beaten. I was too tired to hold back any emotions and I was scared that I was nearing the end. Even though all I wanted was for it to end, I didn't want to feel any more pain before it happened.

"Why are you crying?" my dad asked without emotion. He also felt overwhelmed being around me.

Looking back, I can relate to his reaction.

"Nothing," I softly choked out.

"Kim, don't give me that. I know something is wrong. What is it?"

"My stomach hurts!"

The tears didn't stop this time. My chest started heaving and I reached my bony arm up to my face to cover my emotions. My stomach ached. It had ached all day, but I continued to work, pulling off prickly buds from weeds and then digging their long stocks and roots up.

"Well, duh," he snorted.

He didn't understand. This wasn't hunger pains or a slight cramp. My stomach was cramped into knots, like I had swallowed broken shards of glass, cutting and gnawing their way through my system.

"No wonder your stomach hurts, Kim. Look at all of the coffee you drink!"

"That's not the reason why, Dad!" I slammed my body down in a kitchen chair, rolling halfway across the tile floor.

"I know it's not. You also eat too much pepper and too much damn salsa!" He leaned against the wall and stared down at me, arms across his chest.

"No, Dad, that's not why, either. . . . I'm—I'm . . . sick, Dad!"

My mom had been standing by the sink, being a silent observer. I was shocked when her choked-up voice came into the discussion.

"Paul, she is. . . . Just look at her." She started to cry as she glanced down at what used to be her daughter.

"Kim, damn it, you're doing this to yourself, kid. We have given you all of the foods you could possibly want, but you won't eat them. We haven't asked you to help around the house, and all you want to do is exercise and then exercise some more . . . like you think, 'Oh, I have to do this to burn this energy.' I don't feel sorry for you."

Good, I don't want you to feel sorry for me, Dad. I just want you to see me, I thought.

When I returned to campus after another summer of working road construction and living with my parents, my energy, my body fat percentage, and my spirits were almost nonexistent.

"How are you doing, Kim?" was the first thing my therapist asked me after spending the summer apart.

"Not too good" was all I could say.

"I noticed," she said as she glanced at my frame sitting in front of her. I hated sitting on that small blue couch and making eye contact with her. "Tell me, what do you want, Kim? You obviously didn't get any better over the summer." She adjusted her glasses on her face and looked at me like I was a freak.

I felt like one, too.

"I don't know. I basically have been going in hopes that I would just quit," I answered.

After I said this, she took in a deep breath and set her pen down on the pad.

"What do you mean by that?"

"I mean what I say." My voice started to choke up. "I'm giving up."

My goal was simple, to keep going until I quit. When I was working road construction, I would fantasize about dropping onto the hundred-degree asphalt that we had just laid down on the roads. I could see myself being hauled off in an ambulance with a white sheet pulled over my head.

"Do you want to be checked into a clinic, Kim?" my therapist asked with a straight face.

"God, no!" I quickly snapped back. Even though that was what I really did want, with the hope that my parents would finally recognize I had a disorder.

By the time my nineteenth birthday arrived, I could barely open doors, walk around campus, or sit still in class. The only things I could muster strength for were my workouts and sitting in my single-person dorm room drinking coffee and writing stories. I couldn't socialize with people or concentrate on tasks.

I had essentially lost my life.

Over that Labor Day weekend, everyone in my college dorm left campus to go and visit families or hang out with friends.

I deliberately planned to end my life that weekend.

My plan was to only eat salads and to work out for several hours each day. At night I would vomit anything in my stomach so that my heart didn't have anything to run its energy on. For several months I had felt my heart slowing or stopping while I tried to sleep, so I knew it finally wouldn't take too much for it to hit empty.

On the second day of my suicide plan, I was lying in my dorm room, curled up next to a trash can. I had just puked my evening dinner and was trying to find the energy to go over to my bed. Too tired to stay awake, I usually crawled into bed by 7:30 at night. I could feel my heart slowly increasing the periods of time between each beat. I knew my time was almost over, and I was scared. *So this is finally it,* I thought. A heavy thump pulsed through my chest.

This is the end.

A weaker pulse was confirming my reality.

I'm about to die . . . About to . . .
It's not my time!

My chest felt a hard blast like a paramedic was using a defibrillator to give me new life. I felt a whoosh of energy through my bones and found myself pushing up off the floor and running over to the phone. The first number I dialed was my parents'.

"Hello?" my dad said as he answered the phone.

I could tell there was some fear in his voice. At any point now, they were waiting for the call that I was dead.

"Dad, it's me," I said.

"Oh, hey, Kim," he said with a sigh of relief.

"I want to get better, Dad. Can I come home for the rest of the weekend?"

"Sure, you can!"

I hung up the phone and left the dorms. I walked toward the parking lot, where my car sat. I knew it wasn't my time to die. There was something on this planet that I still needed to complete.

After I visited with my parents and began going to weekly therapy, I soon realized that losing weight was the easy part of this process. Gaining it back and dealing with the anxiety while I did it was hell. While working toward recovery, a part of me was disappointed by the fact I hadn't thrown up the white flag and surrendered my will to my eating disorder. I was tired, emotionally drained, and just ready to go to sleep. I saw death as the long nap I never allowed myself to have in life. I also saw death as a way to end a life in a body I wasn't meant to be in. My masochism took on a new form with each bite of food I took, and each day I let pass by without exercising.

My motivation to get better was pushed further into action after I saw how my appearance affected my five-year-old niece, Kyra, over Christmas break.

"Oh, you kinda look like a boy," my niece sheepishly giggled, causing me to roughly turn the page of my college photo album we were looking through.

I was so tired of hearing people call me a boy or mistake me for a boy at first glance. The whole reason I started the diet was to look more like a woman.

"Dude" was a common reference people used with me, until they took a closer look and then said, "Oh, sorry, I didn't realize—"

I would always cut them short and say, "It's okay."

I didn't understand how all of the magazine models could get by with being skinny and not be called "dude" or "sir" by mistake.

"Why do your bones stick out like that?" Kyra inquisitively asked as she ran her small hand across my wrist bone.

"Just because," I shyly replied.

"Oh . . . you know it looks kinda like you're a skeleton."

"Shh," I hissed with embarrassment.

"You know what?" She paused and pondered for a moment, twirling her pudgy finger through her blond hair. "Your whole body kinda looks like a skeleton." Nervous giggles gargled out of her throat as she slowly picked up a crayon and drew a stick figure.

"Kyra, shh," I struck back in desperation. I hoped no one else in the room heard her.

I don't know why it would have mattered. They all were thinking the same thing. But like the child who proclaimed the emperor was naked as he proudly walked through the streets, Kyra just called it like she saw it.

"Why did you shush me?" she asked with confusion. She didn't understand how shameful my state was. She was too young to understand that resembling a skeleton isn't a way to live. "You know what."

"What?" I asked.

"You need to get a bigger fridge." She added four long lines to her stick figure to form a hand.

How ironic, I thought as I picked up a crayon to join her.

"You don't got any room for food." She marveled at her piece of work before she reassuringly repeated, "You need to get a bigger fridge so you can have food."

Everyone else kept quiet about my appearance. They were all happy that I finally decided to eat again.

♀

It started as a slow recovery, but it would be a recovery.

Recovery was hard for me to work toward because it meant saying good-bye to my disorder. Even though it was killing me, I deceitfully believed it made me powerful, strong-willed, and successful. The only hitch to the success was that it meant eventual death.

Emotions during the "refeeding" process were like a roller coaster. I wanted so much to happen, but it all took time. When I had moments of freaking out, I would go through my closet and take out all the "junk" foods and toss them in the dorm's lounge area for the girls to gobble up, so that I wouldn't.

My therapist had several moments of frustration with me when I told her about different emotional reactions I had toward food or my perception of how my body looked. Her frustrations with me grew as I got closer to graduating from college with my undergraduate degree. She was desperate to knock some sense into me.

"You are setting yourself up for failure."

Her tone made me cringe, and her eyebrows were slanted as she grasped her notepad tightly in her hands. I had spent a year talking about the same thing.

"The weight you want makes you sick, makes you unattractive. Is that what you want?" she questioned.

I sat there for a minute. I was always shocked by her when she got pissed off.

"I can't help it. I'm addicted."

"Maybe you are . . ."

Again a long pause followed, where the only thing moving in the room was a damn gnat that never failed to buzz past my nose. My hand reached up to swat at it, briefly breaking our eye contact.

"Maybe we are just in that stuck place," she said. Her voice sounded tired and helpless.

I had become a broken record always stating, "My outside didn't match my inside."

To express my frustrations I began self-harm behavior with my Swiss Army knife and started to struggle with binging and purging. I kept replacing one form of self-harm with another.

Most of the years I was in college have become blurred memories for me, centered on my disorder and either starving myself, puking, or trying to use alcohol to escape. Even as I worked as an Outdoor Adventure leader, taking groups of people on weeklong trips through the Grand Canyon and on the Rio Grande River, I found myself feeling uncomfortable and disgusted in my body.

When my thoughts weren't centered on my body, they were ruled by the fantasy of suicide. Not a day went by where I didn't want to kill myself either by using a razor blade diagonally against my wrist, stepping out in front of a car, hanging myself, or overdosing on pills.

They were all fantasies, except one.

As I was nearing the end of my senior year in college, I began looking at my options. I had applied to two colleges for a degree in public health, but they were my backup plan. What I really wanted to do was mow lawns and go to school at night for a master's in English. I started to talk to my dad about my ideas on the phone a few months before graduation, only to be told by him that my ideas of mowing and getting another degree in English were cop-outs. I could do better than that, he said. I wasn't surprised by his reaction, every idea or dream that I had was shot down by him because they didn't have dollar signs at the end or they didn't fit into what he saw for me. When I wanted to be a physical therapist, he told me that it wasn't a real profession; chiropractors were better, he said. When I wanted to be a veterinarian, he told me that I would spend all of my time in labs and never see daylight for eight years in college. Throughout my undergraduate years, he was proud of the work I did, but always reminded me that I wouldn't make any money. All of his statements were rational and there might have been some truths behind them, but all I ever wanted was for him to be excited for me as I tried things that were outside what my family had ever experienced. My brother and brother-in-law had both graduated from Palmer College of Chiropractic, the same school my dad had attended. My brother had bought my dad's practice; my sister's husband had started a practice in his hometown, a town in Iowa that resembled Aurora.

When I got off the phone with him, I felt like nothing I did would ever be good enough or accepted by him. As I entered my bedroom, I was depressed, scared, and angry.

A large white bottle sitting on top of my desk caught my eye. I took a second look at it and started to feel calm. The contents in the bottle were Hydroxycut pills. I had purchased them online after learning that ephedrine was banned in Nebraska. I figured the only reason it was banned was because ephedrine worked, maybe too well; so I went online and ordered the pills that were chock-full of it.

I twisted off the lid and dumped the contents onto my desk. I used my index finger to push each one around until I counted that I had twenty-two pills. I grabbed a piece of paper and wrote a note to my dad. I apologized for not living up to his expectations and then swallowed all twenty-two yellowish gray capsules.

I lay in bed for four hours. My heart started a game where it raced and then stopped, raced and then stopped. I began to feel sick; but instead of throwing up all over myself, I made my way to the bathroom, where I leaned over the sink and began to puke a substance that resembled battery acid.

I couldn't stop myself—even though I knew that each time I puked, it released more of the toxins in my body that were meant to kill me. It was my second failed suicide attempt, and my last.

I knew that killing myself wasn't going to make anyone feel better. I needed a different option to free me.

To help me get out of my stuck place, I began to draw using a black roll-ball pen. All of my artwork depicted nonsexual figures. Their external genitalia and chests were clean slates; the only thing they all had in common were their skinny shapes.

I didn't understand or realize until I began my transition six years later that the figures I intently crafted on my drawing paper and painted on my stretched canvases came from my subconscious. I was trying to find my female body in the drawings, but each figure I drew took on a male form.

The more I looked at the images, I knew that the awakening I needed to help me move past my disorder would only happen by acknowledging my desire for love and for sex.

It took me another three years to find the courage to begin this process.

My fingers flowed across my computer's keyboard as if I were playing Beethoven on the piano. I had become an expert typist and allowed my unconscious to carry me through the stories I crafted as my reality. The only things that would bring me back to the world I didn't want to be in were external disruptions like my CD player ending the last track, the landline telephone ringing or the unpleasant reminder that I forgot to turn off my coffee pot. Today, it was the smell of burned coffee.

"Damn it," I said as I pushed myself away from my desk and turned toward the coffeepot in my dorm room. Although I was in my second year of graduate school at the University of Nebraska, I still lived within the small confines of the dorm's cream-colored cement blocks. I chose the dorms instead of apartments because they were convenient for my life, which consisted of going to work, class, the gym, and then coming back to my tiny room to write, read, and play guitar.

I pulled the coffeepot from the burner and flipped the button to the off position before turning back toward the wood chair supplied by the residence halls. I placed a small pillow on the seat to make it more comfortable, but it didn't help. I was able to push past the pain through my constant focus on writing. My stories took me to places and put me inside people who weren't me or part of my life. I loved sitting at my desk with a mug of steaming coffee and my CD player softly playing folk music while I typed on my keyboard. I lost myself in the stories that I wrote; I found it easier to live my life through characters who had the courage to do and say all the things I wanted to do, but couldn't.

As a human I felt stripped of my sexuality; but with each step I took in therapy, I knew it was time to create and define it, like I had done in my art.

I adjusted the pillow underneath me again and glanced over the words formed on my computer screen, a cursor sat pulsing after the word "lesbian."

I had written hundreds of stories. Within each story the sexuality of my characters was never consistent. However, with each creative writing class I took, I noticed an increase in lesbian characters. When we reviewed each other's stories during our writers' workshop, all of my classmates would curiously look at me. I knew they were trying to figure out if I, too, was a lesbian. When someone would boldly ask me, I would brush them off and assure them that my characters were just part of a story, even though I noticed that my lesbian characters were more appealing to me.

I also noticed that at night I dreamed about being sexual with women. I would have questioned the possibility of me being a lesbian more, but the hitch in my dreams was I saw myself as a man. I didn't tell my therapist about my fantasies; I was scared of her judging me.

I also didn't tell her about two very close relationships I had experienced with women. I felt it wasn't necessary, since I wasn't sexual with them even though we flirted, talked for hours, hugged each other, confided in each other, and looked at each other in a way more intimate than I had ever experienced with my previous boyfriends.

To try and express what I was feeling toward them, I would write songs on my guitar and then serenade them at night, or I would write short stories with characters meant to represent us. Both sets of relationships spanned over four years of my life, the increased emotions between us led them both to get scared and abandon our friendships. I didn't blame them. I, too, would have felt insecure by the thought of being in a romantic relationship with me in the current body I inhabited. I believe they saw my inner male spirit, and had an attraction to me, but none of us knew why we felt the way we did. They both identified as heterosexual, and I didn't know what I was.

I coped with my losses by spending several nights drinking large amounts of alcohol and attempting to get high by snorting my antidepressants. After a few nights of doing this, I leaned back against my bed in my dorm room and laughed. I was successful at getting drunk, but not high.

"Is this really happening to me?" I asked myself.

Although I wasn't popular in high school, I was a straight-A student, a dedicated athlete, and a creative artist. Over the course of my college career, I had become a shell that held something I wasn't. I decided I needed to talk with my therapist.

My leg practically shook the whole office as I sat on the same blue couch and in the same spot I had occupied for the past four years.

"What are you thinking?" my therapist asked.

I quickly made eye contact with her before turning my glance away, and affixing it on the wall to her left.

"Nothing," I said.

"Bullshit," she said, tired of my excuses when things got too hard.

I sat there, shaking my leg for several minutes before taking in a gasp of air and letting it out. Sweat started to bead on my forehead and under my arms.

Finally I blurted out, "I think I like girls." I was waiting for her judgment, since most of her clients were sorority girls, who, I assumed, were all straight.

"Okay," she said. "I've been wanting to talk to you about your sexuality, but I didn't want to put the idea in your head. I wanted to hear it from you first, so let's explore this now."

I left therapy that day with an assignment: to explore. My exploration began in the campus library with research articles on sexual orientation. With each week that passed, I expanded my research to fictional novels and then gay and lesbian movies, which I rented from the local video store. One day at the store I found myself looking at used movies for sale. When I wasn't writing, I oftentimes watched obscure movies that felt like their scripts came from a writers' workshop. While looking over titles this time, I found myself zoning in on a film about lesbians, *Kissing Jessica Stein*. I plucked the video off the shelf and ran to the counter.

For the next six months I watched that movie every day. I related to Jessica's insecurities about her life and felt excited by her sexual experiences with a woman. I envied Helen's securities with her body and her sexuality, and I often imagined what it would be like to feel that way. In order to explore the aspects of the characters further, I continued to write stories where I could live a life of fiction, still too scared to go out into the real lesbian community.

I was given the chance to face my fear during my third year of graduate school after being introduced to a woman who would be my office mate.

Her name was Julie. She was a graduate student from the student-affairs program on campus. Her program assigned her to work at the health center for a semester as part of her internship. My boss in sexuality education agreed to be her supervisor. The first day she entered our office, situated in the basement of the building, my supervisor led her to the room I just claimed as my own personal office and introduced her to me. I looked her up and down in the doorway, noting that she was tall, taller than me, which meant she had to be five feet eleven inches. Her fuller figure was dressed in a black power suit. She had long blond hair framing her face and a bright smile. I immediately noticed her voice and laugh. From her projection I could tell she was the type of person who had extreme confidence in herself and would never shy away from making her presence known. Her confidence and cheeriness made me decide pretty quickly that I didn't like her.

Our first week together was one where I acted extremely rude. I didn't chat or make eye contact with her. Little did I know, she was still observing me: the way I walked, dressed, and postured myself. Having identified as a lesbian for the past five years, she had a pretty good feeling that I was a lesbian, too, but she was afraid to ask me because she didn't know how I would react. She already had the sense that I felt threatened by her, so she didn't want to ask something personal and have it blow up in her face. Instead, she decided to invite me out to a gay bar in town with her, her partner, and their friends. I had come out to myself over a year ago, so the idea of actually being out in the community gave me hope. I accepted her offer and ventured out with them that weekend.

The bar was a small rectangle, close to the size of a fifty-foot semitrailer cemented into the ground. It was situated on a dark corner in a part of town swallowed by abandoned warehouse buildings and car lots. As we approached the entrance, I saw a small woman sitting on a bar stool and twirling a flashlight.

"Do you got your IDs?" she asked.

I pulled mine out and handed it to her. As she looked over the dates and shined her flashlight in search of the state seal, my face blushed with embarrassment. My identity had been exposed and I feared everyone would know I was a lesbian. I was expecting her to make some comment about me being new blood, but she just handed me back my ID and smiled. After making it through the first stage of what felt like my sexual identity gauntlet, we headed into the smoke-filled bar.

My senses immediately became overwhelmed by the smoke, noise, and crowded tables, but I was happy to be there and meet new people. During the course of the evening, my coworker and her friends were looking me up and down and asking me questions with the hope that I would come out to them. I didn't. I wasn't ready.

The next month they set up a fake competition, stating whoever could get me to come out would receive a toaster oven. Each time I went out with them, I noticed my identity coming more into place, and I began to feel a sense of community. By the end of the month, I managed to say, "Yes, I am gay."

I couldn't say the word "lesbian." It didn't feel like it fit me. Why it didn't fit was something I didn't understand.

After coming out, we all decided to go back to celebrate at the Panic, our little community bar. We went out to the patio to get away from the smoke inside. I placed myself in the corner on a metal patio chair. There was a flimsy green picket fence, which was on the verge of falling over behind me, but being in the corner felt safe to me and the view of the stars helped calm my nerves. I took on the role my mom usually played and became the quiet observer, listening to all of my friends chat as we smoked and drank pitchers of crappy beer.

My role as the observer was quickly stripped away when a woman walked up to the table and started talking with one of my new friends. I looked at her and noticed her body was small and thin, her hair was cut short and colored a slight red, and her clothing was a little too baggy and masculine for her frame. She looked toward me and I felt a little spark as I saw her blue eyes, small nose, and curved lips. I wanted to know more about her, but I was afraid to make true eye contact, since I figured she wouldn't find me attractive.

My friend Julie, who I thought just a month ago would be my archenemy, called out, "Michelle." It was the new girl's name, which Julie had just learned. She pointed to the empty chair, which I had put between myself and the others, and gestured for her to join us. The woman agreed; and as she approached the chair, my heart started to pound and my nerves started to jumble in my stomach.

There was no escaping eye contact now. We started to talk. In fact, we talked for the next two hours.

I noticed right away that she loved to ask questions. Julie would sometimes interject when she thought I didn't respond with enough information. By the time the evening was coming to a close, we had managed to give the new girl our e-mail addresses and invites to future events. I remember shaking her hand as we left the bar and went to my friend's car. I looked back as we pulled out of the parking lot and watched as she went to her small white Toyota. I didn't know if we would see each other again, but I had hoped we would.

Three days later, I received an e-mail from her. The night at the Panic, Julie and I had mentioned a play Julie had coordinated. It was called *That Takes Ovaries,* and its premise was based upon essays from women describing courageous things they have completed. Instead of saying something like, "That must have taken a lot of balls," the play enforced how it took ovaries. Michelle was interested in the play, but she couldn't remember when we mentioned it was showing. After a failed attempt at reading Julie's tipsily written e-mail address, she e-mailed me.

I was working in the office when I saw Michelle's e-mail address pop up in my in-box. Julie was sitting in front of me at her desk, which had been wedged into the room. She turned around when she heard my breathing become short. I was nervous and in disbelief because I didn't think she would be interested in me. As I clicked on the e-mail, Julie ran around the corner of my desk to read the text and support me in my first real venture into dating women. My eyes quickly read over the content: *Hey, it was nice to meet you the other night. Could you tell me when the play is again, I am interested in seeing it.*

I quickly pressed reply and typed, *So glad you had fun, the play is this Friday. . . . A bunch of us are thinking of going out to play pool before the show. If you'd like to join, let me know.* I wrote this, knowing it was a lie. There was no pool game planned; I just didn't know how to ask her out. She replied, agreeing to hang out, but she was just getting off work so she asked if the two of us could do dinner, instead. Julie sat by my side with each e-mail, cheering me on as I nervously responded to what quickly became a date.

We met at a bar before dinner. I remember watching her strut in. Her hair was short and spiked, and she wore a baggy polo shirt and brown baggy pants.

"How's it going?" she asked as she cocked her head to the side.

"Great, let's just listen to this next reader and then head to dinner." We sat in the bar, listening to my English department comrades read from selections of short stories and poems before heading out for a sandwich and beer.

After we got through our first date, we arranged another, and another. I started to spend nights at the house she was watching for a former professor away on sabbatical. Each night I stayed there, I remained fully clothed and securely placed a pillow between us. I was nervous lying in bed with another woman, and even more nervous having her see or even touch my body.

Two months into our relationship, I had gone to Kansas City for a peer educator conference. When I returned, I helped her with the yard work and then went inside for a drink. She was standing in the doorway, making a joke, and I leaned down to give her a quick peck on her lips.

"It's about time," she said, looking up at me.

I nervously laughed and said, "I didn't know who should make the first move."

We held off from kissing for the rest of the week. On a Friday night I went over to spend some time with her during a thunderstorm. She had just returned from a lesbians' wedding ceremony and so we popped the movie *If These Walls Could Talk 2* into the DVD player. Halfway through the film we locked eyes, blue on green, and then leaned in and kissed. We started to make out on the couch, which led us to the bedroom, but we still didn't make love because both of us were nervous.

It took another month before we were sexual. After I came, I said, "Okay, that's good." I said it because I felt uncomfortable with how we had sex, and I was also uncomfortable with orgasms. I hadn't been that sexual with a person since I was in high school, which had been more than seven years ago at that point. She felt uncomfortable with my reaction, and a little inadequate as a lover. With each day that passed, though, our sex together increased. As it did, I continued to feel more inadequate in my body, but I was too scared to tell her.

As the next six months passed, we started to use the word "partner" to define our relationship. I wanted to call her "my girlfriend," but it didn't seem to do our relationship justice. She had opened up a new world for me; and my heart, which before had felt black and shrunken, now surged with energy and warmth.

When I came out, the disordered eating patterns, which I had been struggling with, lifted off my shoulders and disappeared. I felt affirmed by this awareness, but also frustrated. Although the disordered eating was gone, the negative body image and an interior dialogue that was filled with self-loathing and disgust were still very strong inside me, if not stronger. The suicide ideations were also still whispering inside my head, and that scared me.

I didn't understand what it meant, until eight months into our relationship, when Michelle and I stepped into Calamus Bookstore in Boston, Massachusetts. It was supposed to be a vacation where we got away from everything, but it became the opposite when we came across a book, *Body Alchemy* by Loren Cameron.

The book's sleek black cover reminded me of the silk that wrapped the edges of my baby blue blanket that I gripped in my arms at all times as a toddler. A scent of glue and freshly pressed ink toner entered my nostrils as I turned the heavy gloss paper. Men's eyes, beards, muscles, and tattoos reached out to me. I felt like I was one with the images, like I was home.

"Oh, gross," Michelle's voice rose over my shoulder, her hand followed. Her finger pressed against the page I was admiring. "You don't want to look like that, do you?" It was a question asked in a way so that the person wouldn't want to answer "Yes."

"No." The single-syllable word came out of my mouth as a reflex. I wanted to reach out and pull it back in, but it was too late.

"Good, I like that much better." Her index finger moved to the other side of the page, the page showing Loren Cameron prior to his transition: his shirtless body slim, breast round, and eyes empty.

I looked at where her finger was pressed, specifically by his breast, and then looked at the other page. His shirtless body revealed well-built muscles, his chest was puffed forward, and his eyes were intent.

I looked back at her. Her eyes were studying my face. As a social worker she knew how to read people; as my partner of eight months, she had no idea where I was inside. She shouldn't have felt bad about that, because I had no idea, either. The book in my hands, however, was giving me a pretty strong clue.

With a slight hesitation I moved over to the cash register and purchased the book; then we turned toward the store's exit and our feet hit the cold, snow-filled streets of Boston.

Some vacation. I was trying to get away from life, but life caught up and finally revealed itself to me.

At age twenty-four I finally knew who I was. The scariest part of this realization was the word and label "lesbian" was not part of the equation, but the woman I had fallen in love with was a lesbian who was expressing views that would make her more of a radical separatist who didn't want men anywhere near her space.

I allowed two months to pass before I couldn't keep my secrets inside any longer. Top surgery, as most transgender men refer to it, was the first thing on my transition list; especially, since in the past, I always thought that I'd have to get breast cancer or be in a horrible accident in order for my breasts to be removed.

I knew it was time to talk with Michelle about what I wanted to do. But before I could do it, I had to tell my therapist. From my research on transitioning, I knew that I would most likely need a letter from her before being approved for chest surgery.

"How are things going between you and Michelle?" my therapist asked, picking up over the past few sessions that there was tension between us.

"Fine," I said abruptly. "Uh, there is something I need to talk about." My body felt overheated again. Grasped in my hands were photos from when I was a kid and from my eating disorder.

"Okay," she said, acting like she hadn't noticed the large manila envelope I had brought to session.

"Okay"—I paused—"for the past six years that we've worked together, I have struggled with my body."

"Uh-huh," she said, encouraging me not to stop.

"Well, okay. . . . Here are some photos of me. . . ." My fingers started tossing out the photos in sequential order. "This is when I was a kid and my mom made me a Superman outfit, and this is when I tried on all my uncles' hats and clothes. Oh, and this is when I got my hair cut short. . . ."

I continued to show photos, including the emaciated images of me when I was struggling through the darkest part of my eating disorder.

"Thank you for sharing. So what do you think all of this means?" she asked, her hand gesturing over the snapshots from my life.

"I think . . . I think it means that I am a boy."

"Tell me more about that," she prodded.

"All my life I have struggled with accepting that my body was a girl's body. It didn't feel right, and I didn't feel right. My eating disorder started because I wanted to feel more accepted by everyone as a girl, but now I think it was really because I wasn't a girl." I took a breath in before saying, "I am transgender . . . I need your help so that I can transition."

"Well, Kim . . . like with your orientation, I thought there was something going on with your gender, but I needed you to find it yourself. I don't really know anything about transgender issues, but I'm willing to learn."

"Okay," I said. "I have a book that I found in Boston. Can I show it to you?"

"Sure," she said.

After our session I knew I would receive a letter from her asserting my gender identity and desire for chest surgery, which was reassuring, but I still didn't know if my partner would give me her approval.

The day after Valentine's Day, I sat Michelle down on the edge of our extremely uncomfortable queen-size bed in our shoe-box-size bedroom. I had been zoning out, something I did quite often back then. My eyes were fixated on the eggshell-colored wall, stare blank. Michelle was fixated on me, asking me where I had gone. She was a therapist, through and through. I snapped out of my trance and looked into her steel-blue eyes.

"Honey, I want to get my breasts cut off," I blurted out before turning my head away, eyes squinted, shoulders raised, and muscles tensed.

"That's fine, I'm tired of hearing you complain about them, anyway," she replied, unshaken.

That's it, I thought. *I've spent the past two months worrying about her reaction, and that's it?*

"But don't start hormones. I don't like men," her voice switched to authoritative.

There we go! There's always a hitch, I thought.

I looked at her face, lips pressed together, index finger pointing at me like I was a misbehaved schoolchild, and a sharp stare that pierced through any thoughts I had about injecting testosterone.

"Okay." My voice was weak. I wasn't a very good liar.

I let two months pass again before I had her help me dial the doctor's office where I had chosen to have my surgery completed. I headed out the back door of our house and sat on a warm cinder block. I needed some privacy for this one, having Michelle look at me while I talked to the doctor would have made me too nervous.

The phone rang three times before a woman answered. I was certain she could hear my heartbeat through the receiver.

"Aesthetic and Plastic Surgery Center, how may I help you?"

"Hi, I'd like to schedule a consultation with Dr. Johnson." My voice was shaking and my ear was already sweating all over my gray cell phone. The sun was setting in the west, warming my face.

"Okay. What is this consultation for?"

"I'd like to have male chest reconstruction surgery." It was a mouthful, but I didn't know what else to say.

"What did you say?"

I repeated myself, not happy about the awkwardness I was feeling.

"I'm sorry, could you repeat that one more time?"

I obliged, now scared that the guys who were part of the online support group that referred the surgeon to me had lied to me when they said this surgeon and his staff were great.

"So you want a male chest," she bluntly responded.

"Uh, yeah," I said, almost laughing at the way she put it.

"Okay, then." Her voice still sounded confused. "Will a consultation on March thirty-first work for you?"

I had my calendar on my lap and looked at the date. It was three weeks away, which seemed like forever, but it was better than nothing.

"Yes, it will," I said as I circled the date in red ink.

I hung up the phone and took a deep breath. The rosebush beside me was in full bloom; its sweet smell entered into my lungs before I blew it out like invisible cigarette smoke. I pulled myself up off the cinder block, my butt cheeks sighed with relief, and I went back inside.

Michelle was leaning against the pantry, rubbing her hands together—something she had the tendency to do when she was nervous.

"So how did it go?" she asked.

"I'm seeing him on the thirty-first."

Wow, I thought as I said it out loud.

My transition had finally become real. The moment should have felt cathartic, but instead I felt like a liar because Michelle didn't know all of my desires.

And I couldn't keep them hidden much longer, even though it had only been over two months since I had seen the book in Boston and only a month since I had talked with my therapist about my need to transition. I knew I couldn't slow things down any further, even if everything I wanted to do seemed to be moving faster than a speeding bullet to others. I had waited twenty-five years for these changes to finally happen.

I looked at Michelle, her eyebrows were furrowed and cheeks tight. Instead of asking her what she was feeling, I turned away and walked out of the room.

The dashboard was covered with a film of dust and black dog hairs. Sweat beaded on my forehead and the tip of my nose as the spring's sun heated the blue interior of Michelle's car. It was already an unforgiving spring, a sticky humidity coating the air. The small ranch homes made of stone that landscaped our neighborhood passed by us as Michelle drove us home. My apprehension increased as I felt the car decelerate and heard the sound of the blinker clicking. I knew it was almost time as my body shifted toward the car door while we pulled into the driveway and came to a stop.

I had my consultation with the surgeon and in one month I would be free of my breasts.

I was anxious for the month to pass, but even more anxious to tell my other secret to Michelle. Due to the energy I was pulling from her body, I knew she felt something was coming.

Before I could process what I wanted to say, I blurted out, "I want to take hormones, too." I kept my eyes on the dust bunny dashboard and waited.

After what felt like an hour of silence, she said, "I don't want to be with a man."

Painstakingly, I turned my glance toward her and noticed the tears welling up in her eyes. Her lip quivered as she reached up and turned the key in the ignition to the off position, the engine puttered to a dead stop.

I looked back at the dashboard as I heard her car door open and slam shut. I watched as she went around the front of the car, head hanging low, shoulders slouched, as she entered the house. I took in a deep breath and summoned the courage to follow her into the lair. Her sister was living with us at the time and watching TV in the living room. She looked at me with a "what the fuck did you do?" facial expression. I shrugged with an "it's complicated" shoulder raise, one eyebrow cocked upward and then headed toward our bedroom.

As I closed the door, I turned to look at Michelle. She was sitting on the bed, hands folded in her lap and looking at the ground. I pushed over the messy covers and sat next to her.

She took in a deep breath before saying, "I like breasts and I like women's bodies."

"I know you do, but you still love who I am on the inside, right?" My heart sank. This relationship might not work.

I was grasping at straws, hoping I could keep both the things that mattered to me—my identity and her love.

"I do love you, but I don't know if I can be with a man."

She got up from the bed and headed toward the door.

"Where are you going?" My voice cracked and tears began running down my cheeks.

"I need some time to myself."

I listened as the front door slammed, then the driver's-side car door. Her car engine started and puttered softly before accelerating away from our house. Two hours passed before she returned home. The whole time I was curled up in a ball on the couch, or in our bedroom sprawled out on her side of the bed, sobbing. When I heard her pull back into the driveway, I ran to the front door and waited. She walked up to me, eyes still cold, face expressionless, but I gave her a hug, anyway. Over the next few years, that moment would haunt me.

"I don't know if I can stay with you, but we've had too many good memories for me to just leave, so we'll see what happens," she said.

"Okay," I said. My naivety led me to believe that if things weren't going well for us, I could easily just stop taking testosterone.

With my secret out I knew there was still one thing that I needed to do, something that I had been avoiding.

I needed to come out to my family.

Just two months beforehand my parents had learned about my relationship with Michelle and my then-lesbian identity. After outing myself I took Michelle over the Easter holiday to meet the family for the first time, even though we had been together for a year. Before, I was scared for Michelle to meet my family; but now that we didn't have to act like roommates, I was ready to open up my life to my family. I knew to be truly open, I needed to include my transition, but I wanted to take one big change at a time.

My appearance as a "lesbian" wasn't any different than before I had come out to them. My hair was cut just above my shoulders and I wore a polo shirt, khaki pants, and steel-toed boots. Underneath my polo you could make out my breasts; and when you heard my higher-pitched voice, you wouldn't have mistaken it for male.

My sister avoided making eye contact with us during that Easter, but the rest of my family had accepted the news. They continued on that day like nothing had changed. So now, I was scared to spring the phrase "Hey, there's just one more thing" onto them, while they were still processing everything else.

In preparing to do what I felt would be the impossible, I accepted the fact that my family may very well disown me and never want to see me again. If I could accept losing everything and still move forward, I knew that things couldn't get any worse for me in life.

Days were flipping by on the calendar, bringing me closer to the first big step in my transition: chest surgery. The reality of what I was about to do had sunk in. I knew I couldn't keep my identity a secret any longer, even though a part of me believed that if I didn't tell my family, they wouldn't notice.

While working out in the gym, preparing my body for surgery, I would daydream about going home to see everyone with my low voice, big muscles, flat chest, and receding hairline, and just having everyone do their own thing, where they called me "Kim" and "she," without ever acknowledging a change.

We were all experts at ignoring the obvious, and staying in denial about feelings or concerns. However, the longer I sat on this truth, the harder it was for me to concentrate on all of the things I needed to do.

At that point in my life, I was getting ready to take my comprehensive exams for my second master's degree and graduate from college for good. I needed to begin looking for a job, find the money to start my transition, actually transition, come out to family, and maintain a relationship that was filled with a dominance of tension, while lined with love and confusion. With all of the chaos, I believed my life would find more balance if I just put it all out there for the universe to deal with.

A month before surgery I was sitting at work, going through the websites of transgender men that showed their transition pictures and talked about their hormones, when I found myself opening up my e-mail in-box and typing.

I put my brother's e-mail in the address box and entered into the subject line "Hey."

I began writing the details of what I was getting ready to do, the bilateral mastectomy with nipple grafts and starting on a dose of testosterone cypionate, the hormone that would change my body into that of a male's appearance. I wrote to him about my childhood and my struggles with my gender identity. I described the transition process and inserted links to other transgender men's websites. It took me an hour to craft the e-mail, which was only two paragraphs long.

With my eyelids closed, I clicked on the send button and then opened them to see it leave the e-mail out-box. My hands were shaking and my breathing was deeper than usual, but it was out there now. There were no take backs.

Moments later, while working on an Excel spreadsheet, a blue box popped up in the lower right-hand corner of my computer screen and a little bell whistled. I had new mail. My brother's e-mail popped up. My breathing increased as I clicked on the blue box and waited for his response to load.

I anticipated a lecture from my big brother filled with hints that I didn't really know what I was doing. I was prepared for the worst; even though I knew that out of everyone in my family, my brother would be my strongest ally. His text appeared before me; I exhaled and was ready to accept his criticism.

His e-mail read, *Hey, Kim, I'm not surprised, I've seen documentaries on this and always thought you were transgender anyway.*

My hands grabbed the edges of my desk and pushed me away from the computer screen. I felt some relief and decided coming out was becoming easier than I thought it would be. I went on with my day and slept through the night.

The next morning I was typing away on my computer at work when another blue box popped up. My brother's e-mail address showed up again, so I quickly moved my mouse over and clicked to open the e-mail.

The only words typed were *Okay, I'm freaking out now.*

So am I, bro. So am I, I thought as I began to craft another e-mail to him. He was the easy one in my family. He was my practice for forming the words I would need when I went up against the lion and the lioness. I continued conversations with my brother for another month before I knew I had to come out to our parents.

My recognizing the importance of telling them started after receiving an unexpected phone call from my dad after our visit on Easter. Ever since I became sick with an eating disorder, my dad never called me. He would rarely talk to me on the phone when my mom would call. To have him call me on his own accord, just two months after outing myself as a lesbian, made me feel like something was shifting in him.

"Hey, Kim," he said.

"Hi," I said back, my voice was at a higher pitch. I was still surprised by his call.

"So your mom's birthday is in a couple of weeks and I wanted to throw her a surprise party."

"Okay," I said. During my consultation, when I scheduled the surgery for May 6, I wasn't thinking about my mom's birthday on the eighth.

"I was hoping to do it on the seventh. Can you come down? You can bring Michelle, if you want to. . . ."

I looked over at my calendar. The seventh was the day after my chest surgery. My stomach cinched up for what I had to do next.

"I'm sorry, Dad, but I can't."

"You can't?"

"No, I wish I could. . . ." I couldn't make up a lie, but I also couldn't tell him the real reason why.

"Oh, okay." His voice was soft, and I knew I had hurt him. "Talk to you later."

He hung up the phone and I dropped mine down to my side. I was upset for not being able to see my family, but also for not being able to tell him the real reason why.

I knew I couldn't leave our conversation that way and so I gathered up the courage to sit down and begin to craft a letter to my parents. The letter ended up being seven pages long and read like an autobiography. I explained my eating disorder, my suicide attempts/ideations, my struggles with coming out into the lesbian community, and my realization that all of the feelings I had as a child weren't just dreams, but a deep sense of my true identity and where I needed my reality to shift.

I included definitions on transsexuality and explained the grief cycle that they were going to go through. I apologized for the hurt I would be causing, but stated that I was at a point in my life where they could either have a dead kid or a happy kid. After I re-read the letter several times, I sent it off in a big envelope. The next day I received a voice mail on my phone.

As I listened, I heard my mom's voice. "Hey, Kim. . . ," she said, pausing, ". . . got your letter. Call me."

"Crap," I said.

I waited a few hours before calling her back. Her voice was cracking as she tried to reason with me and understand what exactly I was saying. She kept pleading with me to slow down. She was scared of the surgery I was about to undergo, but I wouldn't listen.

I also didn't listen to my sister, who had heard of my transition announcement through my parents. She hadn't spoken to me in over a year; instead, she would e-mail me and write about how unnatural and disgusting I was because of my relationship with Michelle. When she heard of my transition, she sent me another e-mail, which I liked to joke contained lots of warm, fuzzy statements: *That was such a thoughtful 60th birthday gift that you are giving to mom and dad. WHAT THE HELL ARE YOU THINKING!!!!!!?*

Having lost my patience and sensitivity toward her, I typed back a snide comment, jabbing at the troubles she was having in her own relationship: *Looks like things aren't going so great in your world, either.* I hit send and figured I wouldn't hear from her again.

Feeling bad, I sent one more message explaining my transition and ended the e-mail by typing, *If you want to talk with me rationally, I'll try to support your feelings as you go through this process in your life. But I will not tolerate any hateful comments or verbal assaults from you anymore.*

♀

I went and had my chest surgery, without my family around. By this point in life, I was used to not having them around. After the surgery, I knew my brother was the only connection I had to all of them, so I dialed his number on the way home.

"Hey, Greg, it's done," I said.

"Okay. . . ," he said.

I was disappointed by the melancholy tone in his voice. I knew my parents and sister weren't taking the news well, but I had hoped to receive more support from him. I didn't want to allow my brother time to adjust to the change; I wanted him to be on board and supportive without questioning my choices.

My dad started confiding in my brother about his worry and confusion.

"I can't have a kid who is transgender or whatever it is called. This stuff doesn't happen in real life. It only happens on TV," he said.

The ironic aspect to his comment was that he didn't know I was being filmed by a crew out of New York City that was creating a documentary for the LOGO channel titled *Gender Rebel*. The producers had discovered me after I had submitted an e-mail to them in reply to a casting call for the documentary. In the e-mail I had told them about my chest surgery and my struggles with my body. At the time I hadn't recognized my need to be on hormones, mainly out of fear of losing Michelle, so I described myself as a "genderqueer" who felt stuck between being male and female. I didn't know if I fit into one box or the other. The producers liked how I described myself; so the day before my chest surgery, the director, a woman from South Africa, and her assistant from New York City arrived on our doorstep.

As they began to film, they captured my coming out into the transgender community and my need to start on hormones. They followed Michelle and me for more than four months. They captured my chest surgery, my first shot of hormones, and the day I went in for a new driver's license, which had my new name and gender on it. We became used to the director and her assistant following us around the streets of our city, and we ignored the curious glances from people walking by. When they finished filming, both Michelle and I were sad to see them leave. They had become buffers for us when we talked about our struggles with our relationship. The camera filming our story made it feel like it was just something we were acting out for TV, making the sting of reality hurt a little less.

I wish I could have told my parents about the experience, but I was scared they would disapprove of me airing on TV—for the whole world to see—something they didn't condone at all. I didn't tell my parents a lot of things about myself. My eating disorder had created a distance that led to the ending of our parent-child relationship, and the news of my transition just added the nail to the coffin.

Over the next six months my mom continued to call me, but she would not recognize the reality of the steps I had taken and the ones I had planned for the future. Our conversations became a broken record, key phrases in this record were: "It's just a phase. You were always a tomboy. You don't have to do this. You should consult with us before making decisions in your life. You are causing problems in the family. You don't really know what you are doing. Just wait longer."

I listened to everything she said, but I allowed it to bounce off the wall I had put up between my heart and their protests. During this time I didn't hear from my dad. He refused to call me. He was approaching my transition as an out-of-sight, out-of-mind situation.

In order to help himself in this process and help my mom during her breakdowns, he decided to remove all of my possessions from their house and took the pictures of me off their walls. When I heard the news, I felt completely abandoned by them.

I started to believe that I deserved how my parents were treating me and that I should have been more sensitive to their needs. However, after spending my life basing my final decisions or emotional reactions on other people's needs, I decided I needed to do something my way.

I figured my sister would never see me again, either. The only correspondence I had with her was through e-mail, which she liked to start out by addressing me as "Kimberly" rather than "Ryan."

Shock took over all of my senses on the day I received a phone call from an unknown number.

"Hello?" I said.

"Ryan. . . ," the voice said.

"Yes? Who is this?"

I was confused, not very many people knew the name I had chosen to go by, and the ones who did know weren't ready to use it when referring to me.

"It's your sister," she said as she broke down, crying.

The static and cutting out on her line told me she was in her car. Distraught by her husband's recent estrangement, she was leaving her house with her two kids strapped in the backseat.

At that moment anything she had ever said to me before that was hateful left my conscious memory. I heard the pain in her voice and knew that she needed me. Her calling me, out of everyone in our family, told me that she was ready to move forward.

She drove for three hours before she reached my house. I gave her a hug, noting that her frame was thin, her face worn and pale. I hated to see my sister in so much pain and knew then what she had felt for me when I had struggled for so many years with my eating disorder. We sat and talked.

I could tell she felt strange looking at my flat chest and short haircut, and hearing my deepening voice, but she knew she could adjust. Our friendship began to form as I helped her through her relationship problems, and she helped me with trying to find acceptance from my mom and dad. I was surprised to hear her say that she kept talking to my mom and kept encouraging her just to call me.

After a year of distance between us, I had gotten my sister back.

I figured I'd never see my parents again, until I received a phone call from my mom asking, "Can we see you?"

"What? You want to come to Lincoln?" I didn't believe what I was hearing.

"Yes. This summer has been the summer of hell for me. I think all we need to do is just sit down and talk about what we are feeling," she said.

"Okay." I agreed to the get-together.

I wasn't sure how our meeting would go. The "F" word in our family had always been "feelings," but I was willing to give it a try.

The morning my parents were scheduled to drive up to Lincoln, I felt as if the president and first lady were visiting Their visit would be the first time they had seen me since my transition began. I looked in the mirror to study my reflection; I wanted to see what my parents would see that day.

I was six months post-surgery and had been on testosterone injections for five months. The biggest changes were that my chest was flat and my hair was cut short on all sides and a little longer on top so that I could spike it up. The more subtle change was my voice and the deepening in its pitch. I knew it was changing, since I was receiving more "sir" references in public. That was, until they saw the face that the voice belonged to. The testosterone hadn't yet changed the roundness of my cheeks and the soft downy hair that grew in front of my ears.

I still had a non-receding hairline and I lacked any prominence of my brow or jawline. I knew that I didn't look all male yet, but I was still proud of the changes I had experienced.

In the final moments of preparation before seeing my parents, I squeezed out some gel the size of a dime and ran my fingers through my hair several times to help lift the tops into spikes. I leaned in toward the mirror to see if I had any small dark hairs poking out on or under my chin, but the ones that had started to grow were victims to my shaving a few days ago.

I tossed a T-shirt on over the thick red scars that ran in a slight curve under my pectoral muscles; it had only been six months so the scars were still prominent. My chest was still slightly puffy and swollen, but one would definitely be able to tell I no longer had breasts.

"Ryan, they're here," I heard Michelle's voice through the bathroom door.

"Okay, be right there," I said.

This is it, I thought as I opened the door and headed out to present myself to my parents as their second son.

I went to the front door and watched my parents walk up the sidewalk. My dad was ahead of my mom. His attention was shifted toward the ground while my mom's was scanning the yard and the front of the house.

"Hello," I said as they walked up the stairs toward the entryway.

My dad quickly looked up at me; but as he walked past me, he quickly shifted his gaze back toward the ground. I could feel the tension bounce back and forth between us. I knew he didn't want to be there.

My mom kept her gaze fixed on me and had a look on her face that in the past I only saw when she needed to break bad news to me, but didn't know how to frame it. From their initial reactions to my appearance, I was ready for our meeting to be over.

"Hey," my mom said as she joined us all inside.

My dad remained silent as he glanced around the room and then made his way to the couch. He plopped down in the seat closest to the front door and rested his elbows on the tops of his thighs. I looked down at him, but he wouldn't acknowledge me. I turned my attention back to my mom.

"Would you like to see the house?" I asked.

"Uh, okay," my mom said before letting out a nervous chuckle. She looked at my dad to see if he would follow, but she knew the most she could get out of him that day had already been completed.

I took my mom into our basement so that we could get away from the awkwardness between my dad and me. When we got to the base of the stairs, my mom lunged forward to hug me.

"You know I love you," she said.

My arms wrapped around her frail body.

I resisted getting too relaxed when I heard her say, "You'll always be my daughter."

I wasn't surprised by her comment, but I was saddened by the idea of never being understood by them. I pulled myself away from her and looked into her eyes. We stood there for a moment and exchanged what could have been a telepathic dialogue through our facial expressions.

We were sad, scared, hurt, and anxious.

We were also nervous about my dad's potential reactions, and questioning if he'd ever accept me, or leave that day never to look back.

"Should we go upstairs?" I asked. Without waiting for an answer, I started to head back up the stairs toward the living room.

Michelle had been waiting in the kitchen. When she saw my mom and me round the corner, she fell in line and followed us out to the living room. My dad sat in the same position—body stiff, hands clasped, and eyes focused toward the ground.

We ended up sitting in a u-shape. Mom placed herself next to Dad, I grabbed a spot on the couch diagonal from him, and Michelle pulled a kitchen chair out to sit directly across from him. All of the energy in the room was shifted toward him, but he still said nothing.

My mom broke the silence. "I just thought it would be good for us all to just sit here and talk about what we are feeling. This summer has been horrible, and I think we just need to get stuff out so that we can move forward."

"Okay. . . ," I answered, not knowing what else to say. I never really knew what to say around them.

The minutes began to pass by and my ability to track and remember what my mom and I talked about had turned off until she mentioned my dad's mom. I knew that my grandma had Alzheimer's. She was diagnosed on the same day, and in the same building, where I had my chest surgery completed. I hadn't seen her since the diagnosis, so I didn't know how she was doing, but I could tell my mom was worried. After hearing my grandma's name, my dad looked up toward me for the first time. His eyes were squinted and his mouth was stiff.

His voice quietly said, "You are never to see her again." After six months of waiting, these were the first words I had heard from him. "You are dead to her, as far as I'm concerned."

"Okay, Dad," I said. I felt like I had been punched in the stomach.

"Your voice sounds like a fag," he spat out. "Is that what you want to sound like, a fag?" The vocal punches were leaving invisible bruises on my skin. "And now that we are getting on the topic of feelings," he said sarcastically as he sat up and scooted near the end of the couch. "You don't know the first thing about being a man. When two guys get in a fight, they duke it out and then go have a beer."

"I don't thi—" I stopped short of finishing my sentence by his interruption.

"And you're going to start losing your hair, too. You want to be bald?" he asked.

"I lost so much hair when I was anorexic that I'd rather be bald as a male, Dad," I said.

"And you're going to start getting hair on your back," he kept going, uninterested in really hearing my thoughts on anything. "There is something else I'm confused about." He turned his shoulders away from me and looked directly at Michelle. "You're a lesbian."

"Yeah," Michelle replied.

"Okay, so now how does that work? I mean, you're attracted to women. So why would you want to be with a man? If Joyce decided to turn her body into a man, I wouldn't want to be with her anymore."

My heart stopped. He asked the question that Michelle and I were still exploring.

I waited along with him for her answer.

"We have a lot of memories together and we have fun. It's not about how she looks. It's about the person on the inside," Michelle explained. She still had trouble using the male pronoun or my male name when referring to me.

"You know. I really like you," my dad said to Michelle. I could tell that he felt sorry for her.

"Well, thank you," Michelle said. She looked over toward me and frowned. "I'm getting really hungry."

"Well, let's eat then," my dad said.

"How about barbeque?" I suggested. It was the first words out of my mouth that my dad really listened to.

"Sounds good to me," he said.

The healing between us didn't start until we sat down at the dinner table and began to talk about things we all had in common: hiking, bike riding, and grilling out. I felt strangely comfortable with my parents when I sank my teeth into a pulled-pork sandwich and watched them do the same. It seemed poetic to me to see the beginning of our healing process take place at a dinner table, especially since the damage began at a table six years ago when my eating-disorder identity was discovered.

After we said our good-byes, my mom and I slowly started to reach out and communicate about things outside of her struggles with my identity. Through our small conversations I saw a new transition happening. Our relationship began to change from parent-child to adults: adults who now felt obligated to stay slightly connected, but not knowing why. I struggled to accept the realization that it wasn't possible for my parents to see me as their child anymore. My changing appearance and name went against all of their memories and their photo albums.

Their struggles with understanding how to integrate me into their lives led them to no longer mentioning my name to extended family members or people in the community. I also lost my place in the family Christmas letter, which I wasn't too upset with, since Christmas letters typically only focus on the positives. No one ever writes about their porn addiction or stories about one of their kids entering rehab or coming out as being sexually abused. No one shares the dark secrets and life struggles, even though those are more of the realities that tie families together.

What did upset me was the realization that after I graduated from high school and left for college, I became an orphan. I was a symbolic orphan, deprived of future memories of family events and exiled from celebrations of different rites of passage. I was banished because I didn't fit into the mold that my parents had formed for me. Despite their best efforts to turn me invisible—a superpower my folks might have wished to wield—I was real. I did exist. I was flesh and blood. I was—and am—their son.

I've acknowledged that part of the struggle was related to transitioning in the "heartland." When I began my transition in 2005, transgender issues weren't talked about outside of a small network of people in the community. I decided to change that. I knew the only way we could build acceptance and interests among family members and the professionals who treated us was by building an out-and-proud transgender community in Nebraska. In order to do that, we needed to share our stories and experiences.

PART TWO

FINDING COMMUNITY:
GLIMPSING REFLECTIONS OF WHO I AM

My left nipple is slightly lower than my right. My surgeon offered to fix it, but I declined. Its imperfection is a part of my uniqueness. It's part of the story that my chest displays.

—Ryan K. Sallans

Images from Ryan's hometown, Aurora, Nebraska.

As you drive across Nebraska's state line, there's a green sign that greets you with white cursive lettering that reads, NEBRASKA, THE GOOD LIFE. If you go to a Huskers football game, the crowd, clad in red attire, will erupt into singing, "There is no place like Nebraska!"

The songs and slogans promoting the greatness of our central state were part of my upbringing. I've noticed people who live outside of the heartland tend to stereotype Nebraskans as redneck hillbillies who can only speak in one-syllable sentences, unless one is talking about corn or the weather. I always love to correct one's assumptions of the heartland by assuring them that, for the most part, Nebraskans aren't rednecks or hillbillies; and we don't all talk with a Southern accent.

Sadly, you might not believe me if your views of Nebraskans were based on the movie *Boys Don't Cry*, directed by Kimberly Peirce. The movie was inspired by a true story that ended in tragedy. On December 31, 1993, a young, pre-transitioned FTM (female-to-male) who went by the name Brandon Teena was murdered in a small farmhouse near Humboldt, Nebraska. His birth and legal name was Teena Brandon, but to help with his identity he switched his two names around. Brandon was raised in Lincoln, the capital, and the most liberal city in Nebraska. However, even though Lincoln was more liberal, Brandon felt uncomfortable with the way people treated him, and their ignorance surrounding transgender issues. Over the years, I have read stories and watched documentaries about Brandon's life, but I know that the most factual details could only be given by Brandon.

Stories show that two years after high school, Brandon moved down to Falls City, a small town located near the southeastern border. He chose a town where he could live full-time as Brandon Teena and not have his old identity haunt him. In Nebraska, like a lot of places in the United States, transgender issues weren't understood the same way they are today. The lack of knowledge both by professionals and people in the community made it near to impossible for people who identified as transgender to access surgeries or hormones unless they lived in a city like San Francisco. In Falls City, Brandon presented to everyone with a masculine haircut and wore men's clothing. Underneath his clothes he had ACE bandages wrapped several times around his chest to push his breasts down and make his chest look flat. He also would stuff a rolled-up tube sock down the front of his pants so that if one were to look down at his crotch, they would see a bulge and believe he had a penis.

Things were going well for Brandon until he was picked up by the police in Falls City for writing bad checks. No legal documentation had been changed for Brandon; his legal name, Teena, and gender, female, were still listed on his driver's license, so Brandon was jailed in the women's section; this would forever change his life.

After he was released from jail, two men whom Brandon considered his friends discovered he was female-bodied. Their disgust led them to first assault Brandon at a Christmas party, and then they dragged him out to the country where they raped him. Brandon confided in a woman he considered his girlfriend. She was horrified by Brandon's account of what had happened to him, and encouraged him to report the rape to the police. The sheriff who conducted the interview was insensitive and berated Brandon. After Brandon left the police station, the sheriff didn't take proper action against the two men.

Brandon felt unsafe in Falls City after pressing charges, and decided to stay with a friend in the town of Humboldt, a half hour away. A week later the two men drove out to the farmhouse where Brandon was staying and broke into the bedroom, where they found Brandon and a woman sleeping. They killed Brandon and his friend before moving out into the living room, where they killed another man, who was sitting on the couch.

Brandon's story tends to choke me up each time I recount the details. I know that myself or any other transman living in Nebraska, in the early 1990s, could have been in Brandon's place. If Lincoln had been the city then—that it is today—I believe Brandon would have stayed and lived a life that reflected his identity. I believe he would have hung out with the other guys in the community, and would have worked as a mentor for those who were early in their transition. He may have even attended the support groups that I previously facilitated for transmen, and shared with the group members his transition experience, goals, and dreams.

Instead, I stand in front of audiences or sit behind a computer screen and share the stories I've read relating to his horrific last weeks on this planet.

Every day I spend with my friends in the transgender community, I imagine Brandon sitting there alongside us. When I imagine him alive, I see a man in his forties, instead of stopping at age twenty-one. I know I am one of the fortunate ones, and I feel lucky to have the connections that I do with other people in the community. Brandon was a trailblazer who blossomed before Nebraska was equipped to provide him with support. He wasn't the first, nor will he be the last, trailblazer for the community.

EX-GI BECOMES BLONDE BEAUTY was the headline in the tabloids and newspapers of the 1950s after Christine Jorgensen outed herself to the press. Over the next thirty years there was awareness and interests in the transgender community that allowed people to seek professional help. Sadly, in the 1980s, some harmful research and bad outcomes led to the loss of public funding for transgender health care which caused role models and clinics that worked with gender identity issues to fade away.

After Brandon's murder, in 1993, people in the transgender community decided they didn't want to be in hiding anymore. Black T-shirts were ordered with the printed words TRANSSEXUAL MENACE running across the fronts. The individuals behind the T-shirts also began to film documentaries on transgender issues. By 1995, their actions led to the second wave of transgender activism in the United States.

I wish we could have known you, Brandon. Your death gave us life.

I believe our stories are important footholds in helping individuals appreciate the diversity in bodies and identities that this world should nurture. I came to this belief because of the actions taken by activists and the history that followed.

Just before moving into the fifth month of my transition, I was hired to work as a health educator in a nonprofit agency. Through that nonprofit I began to pull together a network of professionals who were trans-friendly, so that people wouldn't have to flip through the phone book and risk being rejected by another provider.

When I stepped in front of classrooms, I began to share my own story and experiences when educating on gender diversity. I knew that my public appearances increased my risks of being harmed, but I refused to let a small number of ignorant people affect a community's overall well-being. I also started a support group for FTMs and began to research, advocate, and help implement programs and services that would help transgender people access hormones. My work in the community was inspired by the support I received right before my own transition.

My connection with other transgender men in Nebraska started after my boss sent an e-mail to a man named Daniel. At that time Daniel was one of the only transgender people out to others in the community and was seen as a mentor. Through e-mail I had told him about my upcoming chest surgery with Dr. Johnson. He immediately replied with an invitation for Michelle and me to go over to his house for dinner so that we could chat about what to expect both physically and mentally in regard to chest surgery.

I was nervous when we drove down the street in search of his house number. I had never met another transman before, so I didn't know what to expect. When Michelle and I pulled up in the driveway, I saw an African-American man standing near a white garage, motioning us to pull up farther. I was hesitant because I'd never seen a transman in person, so I didn't know if he was the person I was supposed to meet, or someone else. By looking at him, one would never suspect that he had once transitioned, but I knew we were at the right place when he greeted us like we were longtime friends after we got out of the car.

"Hey, welcome." His voice was soft, but would not be mistaken for female. He reached his hand out to shake both Michelle's and my hands. He was about four inches shorter than I was. His body weight was distributed around his belly, and he shaved his facial hair into a full goatee. I was amazed at how the hormones had changed his body into a masculine figure. Seeing his thick and full goatee increased my excitement to start on testosterone. I had always wanted a full beard.

"Hi, I'm assuming you're Daniel," I said as I shook his hand.

"Yeah, that's me. Let me introduce you to my wife." He directed us to the side door of his two-story home, and we entered into a hallway, where his wife stood. She looked like the Mother Earth type; she stood close to my height and had short, sandy-blond hair worn in a loose perm. Her long neck was accentuated by her dangling earrings, and her slender body was elongated by her tie-dye print sundress.

"Hello, you must be Michelle and Kim . . . or Brian?" she said.

"Ryan or Kim is fine. We're still adjusting," I said as I shot a glance over toward Michelle.

"Oh, okay." She looked at me and seemed confused. I later learned they thought Michelle was the one transitioning, since she had a more masculine presence. However, after a few minutes into our conversation, they were able to figure out I was the one having chest surgery and starting T.

"Are you both hungry?" she asked.

"Yes, starving," I said. We followed her into the kitchen and I could make out the hint of barbeque and warm bread.

"Good, because we have a lot here to eat!" She swept her hand over the counter. Fresh green and red peppers were laid out on the cutting board, along with romaine lettuce.

I felt something rub up against my leg and looked down to find a black cat purring as it arched into me. I reached down to run my hand across his back, but he bolted away and around the counter.

"I think he's more interested in being fed," she said. "Let me show you two into the living room. Daniel invited over another young man that he thought you should meet."

We wove through the narrow hallway and into an open room, with large windows lining the walls and cherry-colored wood floors. This was my introduction to Jake, or "Talon," as some refer to him. He was sitting on the couch, hands placed on top of his thighs, as he nervously shook his legs up and down. He was wearing an orange polo with the collar flipped up, and a white hat with the visor slightly bent down on both sides. He was eighteen and just over four months on T.

"Hi," I said as I made my way over to a wooden rocker chair.

"Hey" was all he said back. His lips rested into a straight line between his round cheeks, and his dark brown eyes quickly glanced over at me before focusing back on the hallway, where I'd just walked through.

I felt uncomfortable and hesitant around him, much like I did with anyone younger.

Michelle and I looked at each other, over to Jake, and then back again. The only thing making noise in the room was the clicking clock, which hung on the wall behind me. I heard Michelle clear her throat. She would do this whenever she felt awkward. I cleared mine back as a way to tell her I felt the same way. Jake continued to sit there, shaking his knee up and down. The energy in the room changed as Daniel walked in and sat down.

"I see you two have met," he said.

"Yep," I replied.

Jake looked at me, then back at Daniel, and nodded his head.

Daniel could pick up on the awkwardness and started to talk about his transition to help us all feel more comfortable. I found out during our chat that Daniel was in his fifties and several years into his transition. As he was talking, I looked up and saw his wife bring in a bottle of beer, which she then handed to me. I grasped it in my hands and peeled at the label while we chatted about the recovery process from chest surgery and the emotional and physical changes from being on T.

"Be prepared," Daniel said. "When I started on T, even the keyhole on a doorknob took on a new meaning to me."

Everyone in the room laughed, including Michelle. I laughed along, even though it took me a second to realize he was referring to the increase in one's sex drive. I looked over toward Michelle and saw that her body had stiffened; I could only wonder if she was thinking about me being horny and nagging her every night for sex. I quickly shifted the topic back to chest surgery, so that we could move the subject away from hormones. I knew Michelle was still struggling with the idea of my body becoming more masculine and my voice dropping to a deeper pitch.

"What was your chest surgery like?" I asked Daniel. I looked over and saw Jake express interest in the topic, too.

"It wasn't bad, as long as you don't move around too much that first week," Daniel said as he reached up and itched his chest. "You want to be careful because you could lose a nipple. One of my buddies had one just pop right off."

"What?" I asked before looking over toward Michelle. I could see her face become pale. I knew she had the same image I had in my head at that moment, my male chest with a hole where my nipple used to be.

"Yeah . . . I think he had someone tattoo one on after that." He chuckled.

"Wow," I said as I shook my head.

"Just listen to the doctor and you should be fine."

"Oh, I will," I said. I was scared of what surgery would feel like. The only other surgery I had had was when I was in sixth grade and an oral surgeon had taken a piece of my gums from the top of my mouth and sewed it to the front, just below my bottom front teeth. That surgery was minor compared to having a whole section completely removed from my body.

As Michelle and I left for the evening, I knew that I'd be in contact with Daniel again, but I didn't think Jake and I would be friends. He seemed uninterested in me, and the age gap of seven years made me think we wouldn't have much in common.

A week later, I was surprised to see that I had received an e-mail from Jake. It read: *Hope your surgery went okay.*

Just like the way Jake talked, it was short and to the point. I started to write him an e-mail back, thanking him for thinking of me, when I realized it would be an opportunity for me to ask him about testosterone.

Just four days after my chest surgery, I had gone in for a consult with a doctor Daniel had suggested. I was ready to start on testosterone. I sat in the doctor's office, still wrapped up in the bandages from chest surgery, and felt like I had to defend the steps I was taking in my transition. I began to feel uncomfortable with the doctor when she asked about my desire for lower surgery. I wasn't considering lower surgery at that time and I didn't want to talk about it in front of Michelle, who was sitting in the office with me. After my consult, her office said she wanted to see me again because she had never met a transman who didn't want lower surgery.

Like a lot of doctors I had encountered, she wanted to push me into her vision of what a transman should look like and want. I e-mailed Jake back with the hope that he was seeing someone else. I desperately wanted to have another option, since I feared the other doctor wouldn't prescribe for me now.

Jake e-mailed me back the next day with a different doctor and then asked me more about my surgery. I then found myself replying to him and asking more about how he felt since starting testosterone. The curiosity we both had about the processes we had gone through in our transitions led to a developing friendship. It felt good to have someone else who could relate to what I was feeling.

Michelle was there to support me, but she didn't agree with my transition. She was scared of how testosterone would change me, and potentially us.

♀♂

After a month of limited activity following chest surgery, I began to feel stir-crazy, so I asked Jake if he'd like to go somewhere and hang out with me. He was warming up to me over e-mail, so I figured it was time to test the waters in person. Since I couldn't drive yet, he picked me up in his tiny Suzuki, which had more rust than metal holding it together. We drove over to the mall and sat down with some greasy fast food and talked about how our lives had changed through our transition.

After taking a bite out of his burger, Jake mentioned it was hard for him to be living at home with his parents. He had started testosterone the year after graduating from high school through the help of an older FTM; his parents were having a hard time accepting the changes and the idea of him being their son instead of their daughter. When he dropped me off that night, I talked with Michelle about his struggles at home. She didn't know him very well, but she empathized with what he was going through and gave me permission to ask him if he wanted to live with us. With her approval I called Jake up and invited him to move into our spare bedroom.

I went with him to his house to pick up his bed, dresser, and desk. I shook hands with his dad and looked him sternly in the eyes. I wanted to let his dad know that I'd take care of his son while they still figured things out. With how things evolved between Jake and me, our relationship appeared to have two heads. On one end he was like my little brother, and on the other end he was like my son—a reflection of me. Our house was the first place he lived outside his parents' home. I tried to teach him how to cook, balance a checkbook, change a tire, and other day-to-day tasks.

I also tried to help him shift into his manhood, while I was still exploring mine. I did this by letting him have a beer with me, or by taking him to an adult novelty store, where we looked for things to help ease the discomfort we had with our body parts. We also helped each other document our transitions by taking pictures of our bodies in different poses each month. I had a special folder in my computer named, "T Pics," where I placed all of the pictures we had taken. Each month we would sit down and click through the images and then joke with each other or express our jealousy as we compared our sideburns, bicep muscles, torsos, hairlines, and changes in our facial structures. Over the next year Jake was officially part of Michelle's and my family. Even during the holidays we'd all exchange presents, prepare traditional meals, and then play games like Monopoly or Scrabble before retiring for the evening.

A year later it was through Jake that I met Cameron. Daniel's kindness and openness had inspired me to begin working more directly with others seeking help in their transition. Being in college, Jake had access to other people who were questioning their identity and exploring whether they were transgender. Those seeking information would first talk with Jake about how they were feeling; then Jake would give them my e-mail and suggest that they contact me for more resources. Cameron was one of the people who took his advice and reached out to me. I tried not to invite strangers to my home, so I asked Cameron to meet me at my office, where I would go over the transition process with him.

Upon first meeting Cameron, I studied his facial expressions as he sat across from me in the spare office chair. His lips stayed in a straight line between his small chin and nose, and his blue eyes remained fixated on me as I talked. I came to the mistaken conclusion that he was more serious and timid than Jake. He kept his questions brief and listened to my suggestions. After he left, I didn't hear from him again until a year later when I ran into him at a campus event. I was happy to see that he was nine months into his transition; because he was on T, his cheeks had thinned down, his build was changing, his body fat had shifted, and his shoulders were starting to broaden. I felt proud looking at him; here was another blossoming success story.

He walked up to me and asked, "Can you tell me more about chest surgery?" This question prompted me to invite him over to my house, where Jake was living. He accepted the invitation; after a couple of visits, Cameron became the adopted brother of the household.

Being around the two of them, I quickly learned that Cameron was more the class clown and the prankster. He was the one who cheered you up when you were feeling down. He also rarely stopped talking; this complemented Jake when he was stoic and somber and me when I was worn out. Along with Jake, Cameron was also my junior—by eight years—but our transgender brotherhood kept us connected. They became my second set of siblings. The testosterone that led us into our second puberty and the surgeries that affirmed our bodies as male joined us together and made us family.

Over the years I've noticed our transgender brotherhood and our experiences have turned us into mentors in the community. There are so many aspects to transitioning: the name change, surgical procedures and options, hormones, insurance coverage, legal protection, and finding peace with one's body. It helps when people are willing to sit down and talk about each aspect, one issue at a time.

Growing up, I'd always hated my legal name, Kimberly. I also didn't care for my nickname, Kim. I never felt that my nickname's short syllable ever showed my true identity. In fact, when I heard someone say "Kim," all I could think of was a butch lesbian, an identity that didn't fit me, even during the eight months prior to my transition when I started dating Michelle. Now, after transitioning, I like to reflect back to that time and think of it as *"my eight months as a lesbian."*

When trying to pick a new name, some people flip through a name book, or they ask their parents what name they would have chosen for them, had they been assigned the other sex. For me, when choosing my name, I was lying in bed with Michelle and was looking up at the white-spackled ceiling, daydreaming.

"Sean," she said. Her voice was very assertive and confident. Later she would tell me that she was choosing androgynous names that could be used with females to make it easier for her.

I shook my head. "No, there was a kid in my school with that name, and I didn't care for him."

She began listing others, disheartened by her first choice not being mine. Several names passed before I heard her say, "Ryan." The name clicked. I didn't know many people named Ryan, and it was more than one syllable.

"Ryan . . ." I had paused after saying it out loud. "Yeah, I like it. Ryan," I said again.

Images of my dad's paternal side of the family started flipping through my mind. My grandpa's family emigrated from Ireland in the 1880s. I'd always had a soft spot in my heart for my Irish heritage, including the fact that we were Protestants and not Catholic. It seemed like in the heartland, everyone and their dog were either Germans or Irish-Catholics.

I felt unique being a non-Catholic Irishman, with an even more unique last name. I usually left out the fact that our family's true origin was from France, and our original last name was du'Sallance. My family legend is that the du'Sallance family, comprised of a mother and three sons, fled to Ireland during the French Revolution because the father, a French Huguenot, was beheaded. I usually tend to tell the story after the French Revolution, when family legend then states that my ancestors started the town of Sallins, Ireland, located just twenty-five miles west of Dublin.

Besides the desire to separate myself from those around me, I was also fascinated by the treatment of the Irish in their homeland, on the boats traveling to the United States, and after they arrived at Ellis Island. Irishmen were seen as dirty, drunk, and poor nuisances; they were treated like savages. I imagined what it would have been like on the boats when they traveled away from the religious persecutions and famine, only to land in a country that didn't want them to succeed and judged them based on a part of their identity. I felt strength in my Irish ways, and believed that the Irish blood inside me, tough and strong-willed, contributed to why I'm still alive today.

"What about your middle name?" Michelle had asked. Her question pulled me out of my daydream and threw me into another quandary.

"I don't know," I said. "I can't keep Ann, thank God."

I felt conflicted because I knew that along with my transition, using a different name for me would be nearly impossible for my parents.

I spent the next three months going through different ideas about my middle name, but time had run out to play with it any further. I was getting ready to start my job at the nonprofit agency and wanted to have everything legally changed before entering through the doors and meeting my coworkers for the first time. Scared of lawyers and their legal fees, I downloaded all of the forms from online and read through the name-change process. I hated the fact that I had to publish my name change in the city's newspaper for four weeks, and then testify in front of a judge to assure the court system I wasn't requesting the change for fraudulent reasons. As I was filling out the paperwork, I fixated on the blinking cursor, my first and last name were filled in, the middle still blank. I decided to close my eyes and just let my fingers guide me to the best choice. After I had stopped typing, I looked at the screen and read, "Kim-Scout." I then read my full name, Ryan Kim-Scout Sallans. It was final, long, and maybe slightly awkward, but final.

I wanted "Scout" to be part of my name because I viewed my transition as an unknown journey, much like what life was like when I used to work as an outdoor adventure guide and led patrons through the winding trails in the Grand Canyon, across the wilderness in New Mexico, or over mountains in Wyoming.

My journey was truly scouting the unknown trails of life, hormones, and medicine. A part of me wished I could have just had "Scout," but I had to keep a piece of my past for my parents. As much as I hated the name Kim, I felt it should be next in line after Ryan when reading my documents. I knew if my parents could never adjust to calling me Ryan, I, at least, could tell people they just liked calling me by my middle name.

It took six weeks from the date that I filed my paperwork before I was set to go in front of a judge. All coloring from my skin drained into the wood floor of the witness-box where I sat moments before my name would legally be changed.

The room shifted into slow motion. The voice of the judge was a drawn-out muffle as I looked around the courtroom and saw strangers to my right waiting for their trial. Michelle was anxiously cheering me on from a pew in the back corner of the room, and a staff woman sat across from me, hands poised over the stenograph machine.

"I'm sorry. Could you repeat that?" I said to the judge as I leaned in toward the microphone, but I had leaned too close and caused the microphone to screech.

"You are representing yourself so you need to start this process. . . . I can't do it for you," he said for the second time. Light glistened off his black robe. I noticed his hands were long and skinny as he shifted and moved around the paperwork in front of him.

Now, along with the pale skin, came the urge to vomit. I felt my heart beating up in my throat and a wave of helplessness washed over my skin. I began to second-guess my decision to represent myself instead of hiring a lawyer to guide me for an extra five hundred dollars.

In a moment of panic I remembered my friend Daniel had talked about how he had used a lawyer for his name change and all he had to do was say that he testified he was changing his current name to his new name to better represent himself. I leaned back toward the microphone, right as the judge was ready to give up on me, and repeated what I had remembered. I didn't know if it was the right thing to say, but it was my only hope.

Luck was on my side as the judge nodded his head, asked for my court order, and then signed off on the last sheet. His signature and the notary made it a legal document. In my life I went from "Female Sallans," to "Kimberly Sallans," and now "Ryan Sallans." The legal name change made my identity and my transition feel validated. The court system acted like my parents; its approval and recognition of me as male and Ryan affirmed that my transition wasn't something that I just made up. Transitioning was something that could affect a human being, and something that was legitimately recognized.

The court order also allowed me to contact every business, organization, and financial institution, and instruct them to change all of my documents from my old name to my new one. This included my driver's license, Social Security card, and birth certificate. My name change was my first exposure to the legal system. Although the judge was kind to me, I could see how others might feel they are treated like a threatening criminal, freak, or undignified citizen. I've heard stories of people being denied their name change or being belittled when they presented their court orders.

Transitioning isn't easy. For me, it has felt like the cards have been stacked against me, the only thing that has pulled it all together is my confidence and knowledge surrounding the transition process. Over the years I've learned how to be my own self-diagnosing doctor, legal counsel, human resource advocate, and therapist.

I have learned to be Ryan Kim-Scout Sallans.

My left nipple is slightly lower than my right. My surgeon offered to fix it, but I declined.

Its imperfection is a part of my uniqueness.

It's part of the story that my chest displays.

Slightly offset nipples over faded pink-and-white scars.

To create my chest, the surgeon put me under general anesthesia and ran two long incisions underneath where my breasts lay. Those incisions allowed him to lift up my skin and remove my nipples, breast tissue, and excess fat. After he had removed all the tissue he could, he then trimmed down my skin, laid it back on top of my chest wall, and then measured where my nipples would be placed.

Male nipples are set farther apart and lower on the chest than female nipples. He trimmed my nipples and sewed them back onto the skin before sewing up the large incisions. The surgery took a little under two hours. Forty-five minutes later, as I hazily awoke from the anesthesia, I felt a rush of peace. Two objects that had caused a lot of trauma, worry, and distress in my life were gone, never to return.

Before the surgery began, I was scared of the process and worried about whether I'd be able to handle further surgeries to align my body more fully with my mind. After waking up, I just sat there, amazed and wanting more. I was

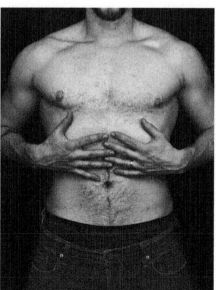

fascinated by the fact that in less than two hours, less time than it takes to watch a movie, my life had been changed forever. A burden that had haunted me since puberty was now removed. On the way home I kept lightly pulling my hand over my bandaged chest while saying to Michelle, "I have a flat chest."

I spent two weeks on a reclining couch as the large incisions and tender nipples slowly began to heal. After the stitches had dissolved, I began massaging my scar lines and rubbing my chest. A month into recovery after a shower, I stood in front of the bathroom mirror and looked at my figure. The chest was flat, the scar lines were small and pink, and I felt male, until I looked below the scar lines and saw my round stomach and wide hips. My body still lacked testosterone, and it made me uncomfortable.

I reached over to the towel rack to grab a T-shirt, but the rack was empty. I realized I had forgotten to bring a clean shirt into the bathroom to put on after I had showered. I knew I could wrap the towel around my top half and run across the hall to my bedroom, but I decided it was my chance to walk around the house without a shirt; it would be the first time since I was a kid.

I walked out to the family room, where Michelle sat with her sister on the couch. I slowly strutted past them and nodded. My face was frozen with a goofy smirk and my chest was puffed out. They glanced up at me, and then Michelle went back to playing with her sister's Chihuahua. They obviously didn't think much about my first adventure out without a shirt on, but I still felt exposed and slightly embarrassed. Being raised socially as a female, and knowing before that I couldn't go shirtless because of my breasts, made it difficult for me to be comfortable doing it now. But I continued to walk past them, toward the kitchen, where I opened the fridge and grabbed a soda. I knew being in the house without a shirt on was safe for me, but I feared other people outside of the house would still view me as female. I hoped that I could fix that insecurity once I had testosterone running through my muscles and transforming my build.

Looking at my chest today, I'm pleased with the results and feel okay with the small imperfections. Chest surgery brought me validation as a human being and the feeling of being a whole person, instead of a lost soul trying to find footing in a costume that didn't fit. My chest became the part of my body that I desired being looked at and touched the most. When I felt beaten down, I looked toward my chest to find the strength and courage to move forward.

Most important, it was the part of my body that touched another when receiving a hug. I loved being able to hug someone and feel their body lay against mine in a way that validates the feeling of putting that last piece into an insanely difficult puzzle.

Even with the pride my chest has brought me, I still wonder how it would feel if my chest blended in with all the other guys. I ponder about what it would be like to take off my shirt at the gym, at the beach, or even in my own backyard and not worry about people looking at me with inquisitive expressions as they follow my scar lines from left to right. I try to push away these thoughts when they happen and take myself back to the symbolism of my body, the story that it tells, and the experiences that I've been through.

In order to become more accepting of my scars, I asked my friend who is a photographer, Fred Schneider, to take a picture of me without my shirt on. After an hour shoot, we selected one of the images from the hundreds he snapped and loaded it into an editing program. Fred clicked around on the image and within ten minutes I looked back to see a shirtless picture of me with a big *T* burned into my chest. Fred then added smoke around the *T* to make it look like a brand that ranchers use on their cattle. I looked at it and found a new peace with my scars. Like Superman's *S* on the front of his chest, my scars showed people a part of my identity, but only when I would choose to reveal it.

I continue to find comfort with my scars by reminding myself that if my body completely hid all parts of my identity, I might forget about what it feels like to live outside the norm.

People will never truly be able to understand the feeling of relief, clarity, and confirmation that a surgery can bring someone who is transgender, unless they go through it themselves. Sadly, the biggest struggle isn't going through surgeries, it's finding the means to pay for them. The professional associations for both mental-health workers and medical providers view the surgical options and hormones used in a transition as medically necessary, but most insurance companies view them as cosmetic.

I didn't think much about insurance when I decided to do my chest surgery. I acted out of desperation and didn't even blink when I sent the check for five thousand dollars into my doctor's office. As I began paying on the loan and looking at how long it would take me to pay it off, I feared that I wouldn't be able to have any other procedures—unless insurance would cover them.

A year later I felt like hell had frozen over when my gynecologist's office called me and said that my insurance company had precertified my complete hysterectomy. I was in disbelief and kept asking them to double-check the precertification code and the name next to it. They kept assuring me that everything had gone through, and my name was promptly put on the surgery schedule for the next week.

Ever since my menstrual cycle started at age twelve, I had dreamed of the day my body would go into menopause and stop menstruating again. Now, knowing it was actually going to happen, I felt slightly sad. I knew that when all my reproductive tissue was gone, I'd never be able to pass on my genetics.

When I had my consult with the gynecologist, she had asked me if I'd like to have my eggs frozen, but it wasn't appealing to me, partly because of the costs behind doing it and also because of the image of my genes being passed on by an egg instead of a sperm. At twenty-six years old, I found it hard to accept that I wouldn't ever be able see parts of me in a kid, but I reminded myself that I had no desire to raise kids, so it wasn't the end of the world.

The night before my chest surgery, Michelle and I had hosted a "'Good-bye Boobies!' Party" at our house. We enjoyed having people over to support us, and to help us forget about the stress that would come with the surgery, so we decided parties were good before any big events in our lives.

For my hysterectomy we organized a "'Good-bye Uterus!' Party." Michelle spent countless hours pasting pink papier-mâché to her carefully crafted pear-shaped balloon. She then attached tubular balloons and two small balls to represent the fallopian tubes and ovaries. When she brought it upstairs to show off her arts-and-crafts skills, we both had a good laugh. If one didn't know the piñata was a uterus, they would most likely see a deranged pink bunny rabbit.

The day of the party we carefully tied the uterus piñata up by the fallopian tubes to a broomstick and then draped the stick across our wooden picket fence and patio swing. I was the first one to take a blindfolded whack at the uterus. Vibrations ran through my hands as the broomstick we were using as a bat crashed down on the fence post, five feet away from the actual piñata. After another full-body twirl, I took another swing and as my stick came down I heard the crunch of paper. I pulled up my blindfold to see that I had hit one of the tubes, but nothing had broken off. My friends, mostly female, clapped for me while they held forced smiles on their faces. I could tell they were all excited to take a swing at the piñata before it was obliterated.

I surrendered the stick to the next person in line and stood back to watch. All of my friends took a whack at it while yelling profanities about monthly cramps and uncomfortable pads and tampons. Later in the evening, as the uterus lay on the ground, torn and tattered, we all agreed that we had never had so much fun bashing a piñata. For me, it was cathartic to release my pent-up anxiety toward an organ that caused a lot of my misery.

The nightmares that I had about my period returning stopped promptly after my hysterectomy was completed. The severe cramping I had that kept me up at night and limited my physical activity during the day also stopped. A couple of weeks after my surgery, during my checkup, my gynecologist told me the biopsy had found multiple cysts in my ovaries and fallopian tubes, as well as dysplasia of the cervix. I took the news as a sign that my body was rejecting the organs that weren't meant to be a part of me. I felt validated by the news, and by the letter from the peer-review board that confirmed my surgery was medically necessary. I watched as my insurance paid their portion of the surgery and I paid mine, but even with the bills paid, I felt very unsettled as if at any moment the insurance company would request their money back from the hospital.

After four months had passed, I received a letter requesting the thing I had feared the most. The hospital did indeed want their money back, citing that "the sex or gender of the patient didn't match the surgery."

I decided to ignore the letter and went into denial of what it implied. They had, after all, pre-certified the surgery and a peer-review board had found it medically necessary. My denial lasted until I received a second letter from the insurance company stating the same request. Another week passed before I received a letter from the hospital showing the amount they had returned to the insurance company, and the new amount that I owed them: twenty thousand dollars.

I knew I had to appeal to my insurance company, but I didn't want to screw it up. I contacted a friend of mine who worked as a lawyer for a non-profit legal agency for the LGBTQ community for help. He quickly e-mailed me back and agreed to assist me in winning the appeal. I spent two months on and off the phone with my lawyer. He gathered every bit of medical information that he could on me, and then carefully crafted a letter of appeal. I ended up mailing in a package, the thickness of a book, to my insurance company requesting they reevaluate their decision. A month later I received a letter back from them; they had granted my appeal.

My victory brought me to the opinion that no matter what, insurance companies should always cover the hysterectomy for transmen. Since my experience every guy I've mentored who has been lucky enough to have health insurance and a provider that is trans-friendly has been able to get the procedure covered.

Ever since the appeal I filed with my insurance company, I dreaded opening the lid to the mailbox and pulling out the envelopes with the documents they hold. My blood pressure rises when I hear the sound of footsteps on the porch, the slamming of a metal top, and the barking from my dogs alerting me to the postal worker and the delivered mail. My anxiousness increases if I recently had an appointment at the doctor's office, applied for a new job, or filed my taxes with the Internal Revenue Service.

I've never known I could feel such fear and anger when opening mail, but it happens every day. As I rip open the top of the envelopes, I fear I will have another letter of rejection. My transgender identity is accessible for any employer to discover. It's down on the books for all insurance companies, and it led me to a medical audit with the IRS. I have become classified as a risk, a red flag, a customer who is denied, based on my medical history. I find myself fearful of new doctors, and I keep my identity and medical history hidden from them, for fear that they will throw me out the door or give the insurance companies another reason to deny me access to care.

The stress that follows me would consume me whole, if it weren't for working out.

Whenever I receive unsettling news, the very first thing I do is tie into my running shoes, slip my black armband, which holds my iPod over my left bicep, and crank up the music, before slipping the ear buds into place. The beat of techno revs my muscles as I head down the street.

My favorite form of cardiovascular activity is running on trails that wind underneath the bridges of the busy city and out toward nature. Running trails is my serenity, trees lined on either side; two small lanes separated by a continual yellow dash, making it appear to be a street designed for clown cars. Small, gradual hills mixed in with a few steep climbs are the minority in Nebraska; the majorities are flat jaunts that cut behind houses and along abandoned railroad tracks.

I could spend days on the trail systems that branch through the city and carry me out through the cornfields, wooded parks, and small towns circling our so-called metropolis. Over the past fifteen years, I've put more miles on running trails than some will walk in a lifetime. I prefer to run and bike, but many others are Rollerblading, walking, or jogging over the different styles of paths that lead us: cement, crushed limestone, or dirt.

The trails are one way that I maintain my sanity when dealing with the bullshit caused by living with an invisible *T* stamped all over my skin.

My other way to maintain sanity is hitting the weights and building a thick layer underneath my skin, which protects me when I'm feeling my weakest.

After four years of working out alone, in my dark, unfinished basement, I took the plunge and joined a gym. The gym is like Disney World to me; there are so many options and so many different machines to play on.

Unfortunately, just like in the Disney movies, there's always that enticing, tempting apple lying around that leads me down a dangerous path: the thought of using supplements.

My desire for supplements grows as I'm standing in front of the full-size mirror, curling my sixty-pound barbell, only to look next to me and see a guy curling ninety pounds, sweat beading on his forehead and grunts leaving his throat. My envy increases as I watch the large veins pop out over his curved muscles. When he's relaxed, his biceps stay full, round, and defined. I look down at mine when they are relaxed and notice that they lose their round shape and blend into the rest of my upper arm.

I'm not man enough is all I think when I compare my body to other men around me. *I need to be bigger. Just two more inches around my biceps and I'll be great.*

I try to shake these thoughts free. After recovering from my eating disorder, I've worked hard to keep my thoughts in check, but images are more powerful than rationality. I know that even with an additional two inches around my arms, I won't be satisfied, but that doesn't stop me from wanting it.

My body image issues and my focus on my imperfections will never go away. They are so engrained into my physique that it's just a part of me now. After thirty-two years of doing it, I'm pretty good at singling out body parts and picking them apart. I feel ashamed of this, especially since part of my job is talking to students about male body image and how the images we see on television or in magazines are not what we see with an average man. I know that the guys we do see as models have the genetics to obtain those builds, and they also sacrifice through strict diets, extreme workouts, and, most likely, supplement use.

People tell me I convey a masculine image, one I've worked long and hard to try and achieve, but my eating-disordered brain prevents me from seeing my true form. I find myself struggling when other transguys contact me and ask how I built up my body, as well as what my workout plan looks like.

I don't want to send a message that my body is what a transman "can or should look like"; when, in reality, we all come in various shapes and sizes, like any man in this world. I want to ask them why they feel like their body should look a certain way to be accepted as a man, but then I click onto my website and the pictures I display over the years. I can't help but think my obsession is fueling their desire, just like when I began my transition and I set the goal of looking like my role model, a well-defined man named Loren Cameron.

The focus on my perceived imperfections leads me to understanding how guys get addicted to weights and their supplements. I've been able to keep myself away from the supplements so far, but the thoughts pop into my mind every day. My right hand is constantly edging my computer mouse toward the search button after typing *GNC* into the box. The battle not to click on the box gets harder with each year that passes because I recognize that the body I want can't be achieved through genetics and hard work in the gym. But I continue to stop myself.

I wish it were as easy to stop my thoughts.

Over the years I found one of the more effective ways to slow my thoughts down and calm myself was through drinking. I didn't view it as self-medication until Michelle labeled me a high-functioning alcoholic. As each year of my transition passed, she watched the amount of beer bottles increase in the recycling bin. I shrugged her off, stating that she never drank, so in her view anyone who liked alcohol was an alcoholic. I tried to convince her that I was just a guy who loved beer and all the conversations that happened while consuming it. However, when I was away on business trips, I noticed that the only thing I wanted was a pub.

The sun was brutal on a July day as I walked the streets of an unfamiliar city, alone. I was in Indianapolis for a conference, which was being held on a college campus sequestered from civilization. I was flying out the next morning; so after finishing up the workshops for the day, I asked where I could get a big, dark, and heavy beer. Some locals at the conference mentioned a brew pub in the "gayborhood," which led me on a mission.

I wasn't exactly sure where the bar was, but I figured it wouldn't take me too long to find it. Following the small hint of grilled hamburgers and faint noise of clinking glasses and laughter, I stumbled onto a large crowd waiting outside a building that looked like an old outpost station. Deciding I didn't want to sit outside, I followed a server through the doorway and entered into a maze. The rooms were spliced into different sections making it dark, loud, and hectic. I looked around the wood-paneled walls and saw license plates, old beer posters, and vintage signs, but nothing pointing me to the bar. So I followed another server, ponytail flinging back and forth as she wove through the tables like an expert biker navigating the narrow streets and cars in the city. As she took a sudden turn left, I found myself at the L-shaped bar in the back of the restaurant. There was one black padded stool open at the turn of the bar so I took it. I glanced over the beer selections, which were written in various colors of chalk on a blackboard, and quickly decided on the black stout. The bartender looked like he was operating with five different arms, his hips pivoted back and forth as he grabbed a clean pint glass with one hand and tossed another into the water pan with his other.

"What can I get you?" he asked over his shoulder as he poured two beers from two different taps.

"A pint of the black stout," I replied, confident in my choice.

Although I was in a different city and by myself, I already felt at home. With each city I traveled to, I always found the pubs that attracted the locals. First entry into the pubs left me feeling nervous, lost, and marginalized; I was the outsider, but typically, after a couple of beers, I knew more about the strangers sitting next to me than I knew about the people I saw every day. I loved to sit on my stool, sip my pint, and listen to the conversations that took place. I didn't love walking in and having the locals who frequent the pub turn around and stare at me, even though I find myself doing the same thing at my own local hangouts. Whenever an unfamiliar person walks in, I study them to gauge if they are a threat, and I observe them to make sure they know the bar's rules. I know how I look at people and judge them, so I feel uncomfortable with others doing the same thing toward me; but I always assure myself that once I get settled and show I'm not a threat, the piercing curiosity will let up.

As I sat and drank the last of my first pint, I looked over at a poster hanging on the back wall that described a BrewFest in Indianapolis. Guys were coming up to the bar and buying tickets, and I quickly became jealous that the city I lived in didn't have the same thing.

"Do you think the U.S. is ever going to get into soccer?" an older gentleman sitting next to me asked. I looked over at him and watched as he spun a small buckeye between his thumb and forefinger on top of the varnished bar.

"I don't know. . . . It may be hard to beat out football." What a guy answer. I motioned for the bartender to bring me another.

"Yeah, I suppose so." He paused as he watched a player bump the soccer ball off his chest. "So what are you doing in town?"

It was always interesting to me to see how people struck up conversations. When guys talked with me, I loved the feeling of being part of the man's club.

"I'm here for a conference." I kept my answer short for fear of him asking more details and then being offended by me. After working several years in the field of sexuality and living in a conservative state, I learned how to answer questions with broad answers, while testing to see if the person asking the questions was open to diversity.

"What type of conference?"

I didn't know how open he was to things, but I decided to take a risk. "A sexuality education conference."

"I got my daughters on birth control when they were fifteen." He leaned back on his stool and crossed his arms over his round stomach. "We didn't want any unplanned pregnancies in our house," he said.

"That's great. . . . Parents are the primary educators for their kids about sex."

My sex education talking points naturally came out. I was proud of what he said and how I responded. There was a pause in our conversation as we both looked up toward the TV and watched the uniformed men run around the field, kicking the soccer ball back and forth. I took another swig of my beer and began to wonder what types of hops were used to make the beer I was drinking.

I began brewing my own beer in 2008. I always joked about home brewing because I originally thought I could easily save money by brewing my own. In reality home brewing is a hobby for enjoyment, not for saving pennies because you won't.

Much like my transition, beer taught me that the things that give you the most pleasure aren't easy and require a lot of concentration. Taking all of your dry ingredients: hops, barley, malt extracts, sugars, and yeast and turning them into a dark hoppy liquid doesn't happen overnight. The initial cooking process takes four hours, the fermenting another seven days, and then the bottling and waiting takes another month. When it's done, your friends come out of the woodwork to help you finish off the bottles in a few days and talk to you about life, feelings, and love.

My home brews have also become a topic that my dad and I talk about and bond over. My dad has never been a big drinker; my mom rarely drinks at all, and if she does, it tends to be sips from what he is drinking. Still, I view beer as binding my dad and me together.

When I was a toddler, he would let me try the foam at the bottom of his bottle, which led to me sneaking a sip from a beer sitting on the table when no one was looking. As a teenager I spent a weekend working long hours outdoors with my dad to create a rock garden. By the end of the weekend, we sat on the porch swing in the shade, arms shaking from all the shoveling, lifting, and carrying, but proud of what we had created.

My mom came out to join us and in her hands were two beers. My dad handed me one of the silver cans and said, "When you work like a man, you drink like one." Unknowingly prophetic words, if ever there were some.

♀♂

I still view beer as helping to give me a manly image, even though most people I've drunk a few with tend to open up and talk about their struggles, instead of talking about women while gulping a brewski and then crushing the can on their foreheads. The problem for me is that the more years I've used alcohol to help with social anxiety, the more alcohol I've consumed at each sitting.

I know that the hormones I inject into my body could negatively affect my internal organs as I age. Abusing alcohol while on hormones would either mean losing my privilege to use them, because my body couldn't handle them anymore, or dying. I'm not ready to label myself an alcoholic, either dependent or addicted. However, I know that if I let another obsession take over a part of me, I'll be joining many other people in the transgender community who use either drugs or alcohol to escape.

I've begun to cut back on my drinking, but have found that I used it as part of my identity. The challenge now is finding other ways to show and depict myself to strangers and to friends.

One way to try and convey a piece of my identity to people is through tattoos. I don't believe in outlandish tattoos. I prefer simplicity when it comes to design and placement. I currently have four, and only plan on a few more in my lifetime.

My most current tattoo is a Celtic forearm band, with the tree of life in the middle. It stands for life being interconnected, which is part of my spiritual beliefs. The green color that composes the tree of life reminds me to take a deep breath when I'm feeling suffocated and recenter my energy on the things that are important to me.

Everything we do on this planet directly affects all parts around us: the energy, nature, plants, and soil. I believe in treating the earth and body with respect because we, as humans, have the responsibility of taking care of what we've been given and what surrounds us. I learned through my struggles that in order to treat my body with respect, I needed to respect and take responsibility for my emotions and my identities. Some may say I have disrespected my body by undergoing surgery, but in reality, a body's respect should come from how we treat our spirit and inner truths. My spirit is male, and in order to live life as authentically as possible, I needed my external shell to show the world who I am on the inside. Our skin simply retells the stories of where we've been and how we've emotionally handled the events in our lives through such things as scars, tattoos, wrinkles, and sunspots.

I decided to put my new tattoo on my forearm, to share another story. I had a part-time job selling houses for one of the more prominent real estate companies in my city. I began working in real estate after I started to battle my insurance company for denying coverage of my complete hysterectomy. I was scared that I would lose the insurance appeal I had submitted, so I became a Realtor in order to have a well-paying part-time job that would cover unexpected medical bills. After I won the appeal, I continued working as a Realtor to save up money for my lower surgery.

After a year of working there, I felt like I was being pulled more fully into the business field. Growing up, I had always been the outdoors kid who took on jobs that were physically laborious, like detasseling corn, lifeguarding, road construction, and tree trimming because I hated being inside an office. It was weird for me to be working within the business world and finding myself fantasizing about doing it full-time and having my identity shift to *Ryan Sallans, the wholesome Realtor who's here to serve you . . . forever.*

Scared of losing my internal identity as an outsider—a rebel who's too risky to have as an employee, I went to my tattoo artist and had her ink me in a place that couldn't be hidden as easily. After the red and puffy skin healed and returned to normal, I walked back into my real estate office, where other agents, mostly in their mid-forties or above, could see me in my tight T-shirt—instead of a Polo—and my new ink.

I noticed their glances at my arm and then back at me, which for a moment made me feel like my normal self because I *didn't* belong. However, my sense of being a rebel was squelched when an older female agent walked up to me and cheerfully asked, "Hey, Ryan, how are you doing?"

Her blond hair was cut and styled for her wash-and-go lifestyle. Her nails were manicured and painted pink, and she wore a pair of khaki Capri pants and a knit top, which were both wrinkle free.

"Good," I responded.

Crap, I thought.

"Hey, congratulations on making it on the 'top closings board' for the month!" she said as she made a copy of a contract she was closing.

"Thanks," I said. When agents were nice to me and congratulated me on my work, it made it hard not to want to stay in the business.

Other agents walking by also saw my new ink, but smiled and greeted me. I then realized that I was more disapproving of working in the business field and having tattoos in visible places than my colleagues appeared to be.

After two and a half years of working in a job that accepted me, but I knew stole me away from my passion, I quit and shifted my focus back to what I loved: public speaking.

Public speaking, which is my chosen profession, is the number one fear for most people. Not me—I fear snakes: Their wriggling bodies, shiny-scaled skin, and forked, searching tongues make me simultaneously weak in the knees but ready to run. I shudder even when I see one of the cold-blooded reptiles on TV.

It's amusing to me that those physiological responses that the mere sight of snakes elicits in me are how many people feel when they're asked to speak before an audience. Unlike encountering snakes, public speaking energizes me. Researchers say that our fears are a primordial instinct instilled in us for survival. I theorize one of my past souls died due to a snake, and another soul was saved by a talk they gave or heard. My life experiences wouldn't be what they are today without the profession I've chosen.

My interests in public speaking began the summer between third and fourth grade when my mom signed me up for one of the 4-H clubs. Female members of 4-H work on their cooking, gift-wrapping skills, singing, and vegetable growing—all the things that would be a home economics teacher's wet dream. Your skills are then judged with the items that you enter into the county fair. If you get a purple ribbon, then you move on to having your skills judged at the state fair. Along with my sewing and cooking, I chose to compete in the speech contest that first year. I was intimidated by the idea of being in front of an audience, but I liked to try new things and challenge myself. The experience was a little more nerve-wracking than I had expected, which was mainly because my mom was the one who wrote the opener to my speech.

I remember, as a nine-year-old, having to stand in front of a crowd and sing a little tune as my introduction into my speech: "All I want for Christmas is a pu-uhh-pee." My mom mouthed along with me, proud of her creative manipulation of the song "All I want for Christmas Are My Two Front Teeth." The humiliation from the tacky line stuck with me up through the announcement that I had won first place. When the judges announced my name, I decided speaking, even if I felt embarrassed or insecure from it, wasn't all that bad. The five-dollar prize that came with the win wasn't all that bad, either. Instead of spending my winnings, I put it into my savings account. (My frugality is also one of the reasons I've been able to take the steps in my physical transition from female-to-male more quickly than some.)

As an adult, I notice that droplets of sweat sometimes bead on my forehead or seep from under my arms when I'm a solitary entity in front of a room filled with inspecting faces. I occasionally forget that the audience members' facial expressions aren't meant to be disrespectful. I remind myself that my feelings of discomfort and overexposure are just an occupational hazard.

$$\female\male$$

Since I began my transition, I've been invited to universities and television shows across the nation to speak about my journey from male-minded, female-bodied to male-minded, male-bodied. My audiences are different, but the questions are the same.

I'm reminded of this as I present at a college on the upper-east coast, a half day's travel from where I reside in Nebraska.

"Hello, everyone, my name is Ryan Sallans. I'm a public speaker and a female-to-male transsexual."

The further into the transition I get, the more conflicted I feel saying the term "female-to-male" out loud. I fear others will visualize the same thing I do when saying or hearing that term: woman, vagina, breasts, long hair, and makeup who sheds her attitude, personality, and skin into that of a man who has muscles, a hairy body, and a penis.

The audience remains quiet after my introduction. I can tell they are curious as they sit there, still unsure of where I am taking them and what a female-to-male transsexual really is.

"When I say I am F-to-M, I mean I was assigned female at birth, but psychologically I've always identified as male. I am here tonight to share my journey with all of you and hopefully help you understand more about how diverse we truly are as humans."

I put my left hand in the pocket of my faded jeans and run my right over my chest, feeling my pectoral muscles under my V-neck T-shirt. I wear clothes that contour my physique for reassurance and comfort. My physical appearance is a sign of my dedication in the gym, and a slight obsession. After hating my body for the majority of my life, I've found it's hard not to obsess about how it looks to others.

"In 2005, I began my transition so that my physical body matched my gender identity. I am now what some call a post-op FTM transsexual, which means I've completed all surgeries." My words run down the dropped jaws, bouncing off their bodies, back to where I stand at the front of the room.

"Uh, excuse me," a young black woman blurts out before raising her hand. (I love audience interruptions. I feed off their energy like I hope they do mine.) "So you mean *you* used to be female?"

"Yes." I pause as I reach up and adjust my green-rimmed glasses, pressing on the middle so that they moved farther up my nose. This is a habit I picked up from watching the Clark Kent character in the *Superman* movies. As I warm up more to the audience, I find my awkward habits start to decrease.

"Wow, I would've never guessed it. . . . You look all male to me." She looks me up and down. "You're really hot," she assesses.

"Thank you," I respond. I feel a warm sensation rush into my cheeks and know I can't stop myself from blushing.

When I share my story, I often find myself turning off any filters that I have, so that the audience can ask any question they want and receive an answer. In reality, I could go "stealth" and never out myself as "trans," but I believe I've been given a talent and have found that my story has helped others from around the world. My friends always marvel at how I can get up in front of a room full of strangers and be so open, especially since I tend to be private and shy around people I don't know well. I have noticed that when I speak, I take on the persona of transman Ryan; and I am confident, articulate, and approachable. When I'm off the clock, I am still approachable, but I find myself going back to being more quiet, uncertain, and shy.

"Do you sometimes miss being a woman?" a young man asks. His black hair has been cut into a Mohawk and the light shimmers off his silver piercings, which poke through both nostrils and his lower lip.

"No." I take in a breath. The sharp scent of dry-erase markers enter my nostrils; I miss the fullness of dusty chalk.

"Imagine looking down at your body right now and seeing breasts and a vagina. How would you feel?" My dry humor starts to play a role in helping people understand how it may feel to be transgender. "Sure, you may want to play with the breast for a little bit, but after the novelty of that wears off, you might feel a little"—I pause—"off."

The class laughs; the Mohawk nods up and down; I move on. The age-old question is always brought up during the end of my talks, if I had forgotten to bring it up earlier.

A woman is usually the one to raise her hand and ask, "How is your relationship with your partner? Are you still together?"

I'll look up toward the ceiling while flashbacks flip through my mind and ultimately land on one of the life-changing moments in my relationship.

PART THREE

FINDING IDENTITY:
FINDING MYSELF

I took a step back and looped around the other men and walked over by my dad. He looked down toward me and patted my shoulder. My dad's gesture made me feel that Grandma's death reincarnated my birth into the family. This time I didn't come out as their daughter, but as their second son.

—Ryan K. Sallans

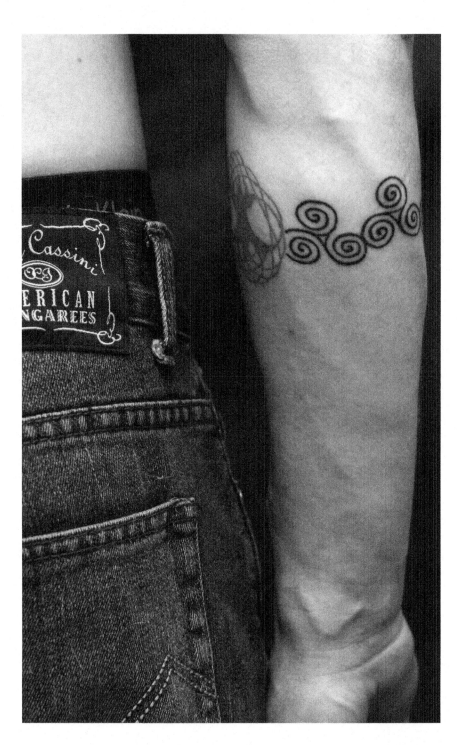

Christmas, 2005, had passed. The ranch-style stone house I was renting with Michelle was still illuminated by our live-cut, eight-foot Christmas tree, which we had purchased from a local hardware store. The smell of pinecones and cedar was still wafting in the air, faint, but there.

Our dog, a boxer/Lab mix, and cat, a short-haired tabby, were both passed out on the living-room couch, along with Jake. He was going on day two of recovering from chest surgery, and I was going on day two of being his nurse.

This is family, I thought as I walked into the master bedroom, where Michelle was lying in bed, reading a book.

With the high from the holidays and the activities that reminded me of my family growing up, I looked at her and blurted out, "Honey, I think we should buy a house together."

She turned her gaze away from her book and toward me.

I was hoping for a smile and a gleeful response, like what you would see in one of those corny Christmas movies. Instead, her face was somber, lips pressed shut.

"No," she said. "I don't want change."

The eggnog I had drunk earlier began turning in my stomach. I was always trying to play out the romantic traditions I had stored in my mind. I wanted my life and my relationship to mirror that of my parents and the characters I had created in my short stories. Even though I didn't want kids, I had images of Michelle and me sitting in rocking chairs and sharing stories about our life together, like my mom and dad had shared with me. I always thought that if I gave everything I had, falling in love would be easy and welcomed. In our relationship, however, it appeared that my idealized romance would never come to fruition.

I believed that because of my transition, Michelle held the trump card over me and what we could define as "ours," since she was sacrificing pieces of her lesbian identity to stay with me.

With each big step we took, I knew I would have to struggle between balancing my raw emotions and her fear to commit fully, but I didn't back down. I took a step back from the bed, put my hands in my pocket, and lifted my shoulders while tilting my head.

My voice of reason started to come out. "You know . . . with the amount we are paying for rent, we could have a home that we're building equity in."

"No, I don't want to," she said as tears started dripping down her cheeks. She moved her book back in front of her face, but I knew she wasn't really reading.

I left the room, feeling unloved. I wound through our kitchen and down the stairs into our dark basement. I sat alone on the futon mattress tossed on the floor. My tabby cat, P.J., slid down the stairs and rounded the corner. She let out a small meow as she rubbed up against my leg. I felt the vibrations from her purring as she arched her back into my hand.

I knew that if Michelle gave me a chance, we could have a home together and further our commitment to each other. I looked over to our bookshelf and reached out for a black leather picture album. I flipped open the cover and was greeted by images of Michelle and me when we first started to date. Both of our faces were tense as we posed. My arm was behind her shoulders, and my hair was long, straight, and hanging in my face. I had my hand clasped on a bottle of Bud Light; she had hers wrapped around a glass of soda.

As I kept flipping the pages of the album, the tension in our faces moved toward being more relaxed as the first few months passed, then to tense again when I started my transition, and back to relaxed, after making it through the first year.

Prior to my transition she had held me as I cried, chest heaving as I laid my head in her lap. I had cried about my parents and my feelings of abandonment; I had cried out of fear of them accepting my relationship with a woman; I had cried because I didn't know why I felt alien in my body.

When I began my transition and entered my second puberty, she was there for each new and exciting change that my body experienced. When I went to the hospital to undergo a surgical procedure, she waited, alone, outside the operating rooms, while I was under the knife; and she took care of me when I was recovering. Not only did she help nurse me back to health, but she was there to hold me as I had more emotional reactions to talks with my parents or my sister. Through all the moments we had together that I felt increased our emotional bond, I kept asking her to marry me, but she kept saying no.

I sat downstairs for a couple of hours looking at the images and questioning if I wanted the house as a financial investment, or if I wanted it to cement our relationship. After coming to the decision that I wanted a house for both reasons, I pushed myself up from the hard mattress and headed back upstairs.

I wound back through the kitchen and living room, where our friend Jake was still passed out on the reclining couch; blue Jell-O he'd vomited up earlier had stained his lips. I slowly crept by so that I wouldn't wake him from his drugged slumber, and I timidly pushed the door to our bedroom back open. Michelle looked up from her book, a box of tissues sat next to her with several used ones crumpled on her lap.

"You know," I said, ignoring her puffy face and annoyed glances, "perhaps we could just go and look. Just because we look at homes doesn't mean we have to buy one," I rationalized.

She stared at me for a minute before giving me a look that said, "If this shuts you up, fine."

A week later we put an offer down on a home. The month after that, we moved in.

Our first month in our new home was like something you'd see in the movies. We worked night and day painting rooms and arranging furniture. We ate picnics on the floor while waiting to pick up a dining-room table and chairs. We chased each other around different rooms with dripping paintbrushes. We were a young couple in love and excited by the reality of owning a home.

The second month of homeownership, we separated.

Right after we purchased our house, Michelle started a new job working as a case manager for a nonprofit. A lot of her new coworkers were self-identified lesbians. Looking at Michelle, her short spiky hair, clothing from the boys' section and tennis shoes, one would assume she was a lesbian, too. She envied the women at her work, and felt ashamed to talk about her relationship with me. I became known as her partner: no name and no pronouns were used.

Along with not seeing herself reflected in the women she worked with, she was having problems adjusting to the new work demands and mounds of paperwork. For someone who didn't like change, my transition, her job, and our new home engulfed her with a sense of nowhere to escape. I picked up on her stress, but kept reassuring her that it took time to adjust to a new job. Her head nodded in agreement; her body, with knees pulled up to her chest, expressed doubt.

After a few weeks at her job, she decided to join a softball team to help her with stress relief. When she was home, I noticed her cell phone started to ring more often than usual. At first, I thought the calls were from people at her work, so I shrugged them off. My shrugs stopped after another week of noticing she wasn't coming home until later in the evening.

When she was home, she'd sneak away to take phone calls outside. One night I watched her through the kitchen window. I had noticed that whenever she took a work call, she would pace back and forth or use a lot of hand gestures while speaking with the person on the other line. Tonight she sat, relaxed, on the patio swing and lazily pushed herself back and forth. I quickly stepped away from the window and began washing the dishes that had piled up on the counter. As I scraped at the burned meat on the bottom of a frying pan, I heard the back door squeak open. Our dog's paws thundered up the stairs, carrying her into the kitchen. Michelle's footsteps followed.

"Who were you talking to?" I asked.

"Just someone from the softball team," she quickly replied.

"Who?" I prodded.

"Just someone named Ellen." She set her phone down on the counter and reached for a glass to fill with water.

I watched her lean over and pull up on the handle to the faucet; she then walked away with her glass. As she passed the counter, my eyes caught the shimmer of light off her cell phone's silver casing. My pulse rose as I listened for her steps up the stairs and heard the door close to our bathroom. Without thinking, I snatched up her phone. My thumbs worked quickly, pressing through the menus until I reached the call history. I looked through the list and noticed the number she had just spoken with.

Later that week I received the phone bill in the mail. My fingers fumbled to tear open the envelope and flip through the pages of call histories. I felt a lump in my throat as I saw the same number in her call history popping up over and over again. Calls were received and sent out at all hours of the day, including after I went to bed at night. My face went pale and I started to feel off balance. I fell down onto the floor next to our table, with the papers scattered around me.

That evening I sat in my recliner and waited for her to come home. As she entered the door, I could feel her emotions toward me were shut down.

"Where were you?" I asked.

"Just out having coffee with Ellen," she said as she tossed her green bag in the corner by our shoes.

I had picked up all of the papers I had dropped earlier, folded them, and placed them in a drawer in my office.

"You sure do have coffee with her a lot."

"It's nice to talk to someone else in the community. It's helping me adjust to how my identity has changed since you started your transition," she said as she walked away from me and around the corner into the kitchen.

"Okay," I said, shying away from further confrontation and digging for more information.

The next night I waited for her to come home for dinner. She had been off from work for an hour, so I knew she wasn't late due to traffic. I picked up my phone and held down the number one on my speed dial. Her phone kept ringing and going to voice mail, but I kept calling every ten minutes until she picked up.

"Hello," she said, her voice sounded annoyed.

"Where are you?"

"I'm out having coffee. I'll be home later."

"What time is later? I have dinner ready." I leaned over the kitchen sink and pressed my head against the window, the glass cooled the rising temperature I felt rushing over my forehead.

"I don't know. . . . Just go ahead and eat without me."

"Fine," I said. We both hung up the phone.

An hour later I saw her headlights flash across the living room's walls; the sun had set for the evening.

I called for my dog and let her outside, where I then stood waiting. I heard Michelle's car door slam and then her fingers fumbling with the gate. I walked over to the lock and looked through the gaps between the wood pickets.

"Are you cheating on me?" I asked. It was the most direct and bold I had ever been with her.

"No," she scoffed.

I knew she was lying. Her eyes were wide open and her lips were curled up as if she found my question humorous.

"Liar," I said as I walked away from the gate and threw myself onto our patio swing.

She hesitated before walking past the gate and into the backyard; she gently sat down next to me. I could feel tears pushing into my eyes, but I tried to hold them back.

"There is someone." Her voice was soft and calm. She did this when she was talking about something that was hard for her to communicate.

"Is it Ellen?" I asked in a rhetorical way.

"I am attracted to her, yes."

"How could you do this to me . . . to us? We just bought this stupid house!" I threw my head back and rested it on the cushion behind me. I kept my gaze fixated on the dim twinkle of the Big Dipper. I wanted to revert back to being a kid, hanging out in my pasture—just me, the stars, and nature.

"It's just hard for me. . . ," she paused. "I'm at a job where most of the women are lesbians. I don't feel like I fit into my own community anymore." She pressed her feet on the ground as a brake, stopping the swing on its way back down. "There is an intense attraction between Ellen and me, and I feel like I need to explore it, and . . . I want to go out with her this weekend for a hike."

"Are you crazy?!" Unlike her, my voice was not soft or calm.

"I'm going to do it. I need to."

"Fuck you," I said while jumping up from the swing. I needed to get away from Michelle.

Still in a daze, I waited for her to come home again the next night for dinner. I had attempted to call her phone, but it went directly to voice mail. My face started to perspire and I felt all the air in my lungs forming a geyser, only to bottleneck in my throat. I leaned over and dropped my hands to my knees. I had choked on the air and was holding back the desire to vomit.

Fuck this, I thought as I scooped up my keys from the dining-room table and ran out the front door, unsure if I had locked it. I jumped into my blue Chevy pickup and stuck my key in the ignition. My engine barely puttered to a start before I pressed my foot on the accelerator and started driving.

I decided to hit every coffee shop in town, starting with the one closest to our house. I sped down the side streets and wove between cars on the two-lane road. I heard some cars honk at me but didn't pay attention. I was in no shape to be on the road. I wasn't paying attention to anything ahead of me. Instead, I found myself focusing on images in my head that were playing out how I would react to Michelle when I found her. There was no sign of her car in the parking lot of the first coffee shop, so I started on the road toward the next.

As I reached an intersection a half mile from my next stop, I looked over and saw her white SUV parked at a gas pump. I swerved past the cars behind me, ignoring the use of my blinker, and pulled up next to her. She was sitting in the driver's seat with her window rolled down. Her left arm was dangling out the window and her leg was bent up next to her body. She was singing as she looked over and saw me roll down my passenger-side window. My eyes pierced through her body. Her mouth stopped short of sounding the next word in the verse she was imitating.

"What are you doing?!" I yelled.

I had never felt that much passion and hatred radiate at the same time from my body.

"What are *you* doing?" she asked while releasing her relaxed pose and sitting upright in her car. "Go home."

"Is that bitch inside? Is she with you?" I gripped the steering wheel. The hard, ribbed plastic became part of my hands. I felt like I had become possessed, using language and gestures that were outside of my character.

"Ryan, go home," she ordered. "I will be there shortly." She glanced over her shoulder, searching for any sign of Ellen approaching the car.

"Fine! See you there," I spat before speeding off. The tone in her voice pushed me closer to my more passive self.

More cars honked at me as I wove back to the house. I pulled up in front and got out of my truck. My legs only had the energy to carry me to the porch, where I leaned against the railing and waited for her return. I waited for a half hour before I saw her car slowly pull in behind mine. Michelle looked at me from behind the steering wheel before turning the engine off. I watched with rage as she walked up the sidewalk and onto our porch.

Even with my rage I wanted to reach out and hug her. I yearned for human touch; but I knew if I did, she wouldn't return the feelings I needed. For the past week, each time I tried to hug her, she'd go limp with her arms to her side. I would say that I loved her, and she would turn her head away as if she hadn't heard me. She was completely cold. I knew she was done.

"You really don't love me anymore?" I asked.

Michelle rocked back and forth on the porch swing, focused dead ahead, away from me.

"Look at me!" I yelled, aware that the neighbors could hear us but unconcerned about what they thought. "Why don't you just look at me and see me?" I pleaded.

Annoyed, she turned her head toward me and made eye contact.

"You keep saying that I'm 'just a man now,' but I am the same person you fell in love with before," I pointed out.

"It's different now," she said. She lifted herself off the swing and turned to go back inside.

I followed and started to ramble. "Do you want me out? Do you want to go and sleep with her? Fine, go sleep with her! Get it out of your system."

She had walked over to our couch and threw herself over the cushions.

I continued forward and stormed up the stairs. I swung open the closet door and pulled out my suitcase; then I went over to our dresser and, without paying attention, scooped up a bunch of items, tossing them into the suitcase's black cavity. I stormed back down the stairs and looked over at her. She sat up and looked at me, then down to what I was carrying.

"Where are you going?" she quietly asked.

"I don't know yet." I reached over for my wallet and keys. My face was puffy from crying, and so I grabbed my white ball cap and pulled it down on my forehead.

Michelle got up off the couch and for the first time in a week voluntarily hugged me. I squeezed her small frame against my chest, hoping to hear her say, "Stay."

After a brief moment I lost that hope.

"I'll call you tomorrow," I said before slamming the door shut behind me.

I ended up in the spare bedroom at my friend Julie's house. It was ironic for me to be staying in the house of the person who hooked me up with Michelle in the first place. With all the things I had gone through in my life, I had never felt as broken and psychotic as I did at that moment. I made it through the week with limited phone conversations with Michelle; however, I cracked that Saturday morning and believed that if she just saw how pathetic I looked, she would stay with me.

As I swung the door open to the front of our house, I was greeted by our cat's gleaming eyes. I walked past her and went up the stairs. The door to our bedroom was cracked open. I swung it the rest of the way open and looked down at Michelle sleeping. I debated whether I wanted to shake her or not; she had always been a heavy sleeper.

"Michelle," I whispered. I slowly approached the bed and sat on the corner. My voice cracked as I said, "Wake up."

She slowly turned toward me, her eyes half open and blinking.

"Ryan, what are you doing here?" she asked.

"I just want to talk," I said.

She rolled back to her side. "You shouldn't be here right now. Go back to Julie's."

I wanted to stay, but knew that it would only cause more problems between us. I lifted myself off the bed and retreated back to my car. I felt ruined.

After a few more days, Michelle moved into her mom's house so that I could return to our bedroom. She started to see a therapist in order to gain some guidance. I waited that week for her to call me. When she did, I could tell it wouldn't be a long phone conversation.

"I've talked with my therapist and we have developed some ground rules and guidelines," she said.

"What are those?" I asked. I was pissed at the idea of having even more ground rules. Our relationship began two years ago with boundaries and ground rules. The first month we were together, she said I could spend the night at her house, but that I had to sleep on the couch. The third month, both of our leases expired on our apartments, but we had to get separate places. She kept repeating the word "boundaries" and the magic number "nine months," before we could live together. After two years together, I had become accustomed to her terms, and felt sneaky when she would agree to suggestions I made about steps we should take in our relationship.

"We can talk twice a week, for an hour each time, and on the weekends we can go out one day for a few hours, but that's it."

"Really?" I asked in disbelief.

"Those are what I'm currently comfortable with," she said. "You can call me Wednesday, if you want."

The time I spent alone with my thoughts led me to further distress. I decided that I needed to be what she wanted, so I started to shave every part of my body and began to reduce how much testosterone I was injecting.

When I came into contact with my friends, I described how I was planning to go off testosterone, revert back to my old name, and live my life as genderqueer. They all looked at me with disbelief and sadness.

"That's just not who you are" became their repeated phrase.

I refused to listen to my friends; my mind was already made up. When I went into my doctor's office and started to talk with her about how I had lowered my dose of testosterone, she looked at me with sheer confusion.

"Why would you want to do that?" she asked. She was a stocky woman with gray hair that hung angular and straight.

"Because my girlfriend left me," I said.

"Well, then, it sounds like you need a new girlfriend," she said matter-of-factly as she shook her head and straightened her back. She then rolled her stool over toward the wall to grab the ear and nose scope.

The brief moment of silence allowed me take in her directness. I felt something rush over me that I hadn't felt before. In front of me was practically a stranger, but she was one of the first people I felt really saw me. She had just validated my identity as Ryan and put the idea in my head that Michelle wasn't the only person in the world who would ever be with me.

I went home that day with images of me being independent and single. I fantasized about meeting a feminine woman who would desire my flat chest and stubbly chin. I began to wonder what it would be like not to have to apologize for my body and my identity as a male.

It was a fantasy I was ready to move forward with, but then quickly left it behind when Michelle called me up and asked if I would be willing to go to couple's therapy with her.

We had been separated for a month and she missed me like I missed her.

♂

After three sessions of hearing the therapist say to Michelle that it sounded like she just wanted to be with women, and that it wouldn't work with me because I was a man, I had had enough. Instead of going back and paying her another seventy-five dollars, I suggested that we take a vacation and see how we felt being with each other. I knew she loved the mountains, so we drove eight hours to Boulder, Colorado, where we could escape on the hiking trails that cut through the Rockies.

The motel we checked into was built in the 1970s and was nestled among the other stores in downtown Boulder. There were only two stories to the motel, which was in the shape of a U, and the only way to access your room was from the outside. Doors swung open and offered a peek inside to everyone in the parking lot or driving by. The room we had was right next to the pool, which really should have been classified as a hot tub due to its size. The humidity from the pool had seeped through the large window causing moisture damage through the room; mold speckled the ceiling, and the wallpaper was curling on top of itself in the corners. The sad state of the motel fit well with how we were feeling about each other.

I watched as she tossed her suitcase on the queen-size bed, and I began to wonder how she would feel sleeping next to me again. Before she had distanced herself from me, we would fall asleep with her legs draped over mine. In the morning we would squeeze our arms around each other, or rub each other's backs before getting up for the day. I had the feeling our nights in the bed together now would be much like it was when we first started dating, pillows separating our sides, and my body stiff and still throughout the night.

"Should we go out for some dinner?" I asked, watching as she rummaged through her bag. I wasn't even sure if she knew what she was looking for.

"Sure," she said as she tossed her clothes aside and flipped the lid of the suitcase back on top.

We started walking toward the district of town that housed all the shops and hipster restaurants. We weren't sure where the district started, so we just walked. The faint sound of an acoustic guitar and whiffs of meat being grilled on the barbeque told me we were close.

I found myself reaching my hand out to hold Michelle's as we stepped onto a street created for pedestrians, free of the horns and squeals of annoyed drivers. Her hand stiffened in mine. She looked over to me; our eyes made contact for the first time in over a month. She relaxed her fingers into my palm. Her small gesture was a sign that we should try to be a couple during our trip and get back in touch with the parts that made us fall in love with each other the first time around.

Memories of the trip were captured through extended-arm pictures; our heads were in the foreground and the jutted landscape as our backdrop. As we hiked on the muddy trails and were pummeled by the rain, I wanted to say, "I love you." I wanted to say it again as we changed our soaked clothing in our car, hoping no one else would see our naked bodies wriggling into different positions to pull our pants up. I decided to hold back my emotions and approach her the same way I would an uncertain animal—small gestures and brief eye contact to let her know I was someone she could trust.

"Will you move back into the house?" I asked as I drove along the small, winding highways that led us back to Nebraska.

"I will . . . but I want to stay on the couch for a while," she said.

I knew relationships took work, but a part of me felt relationships shouldn't take *this much* work. Yet, I kept sacrificing my needs because I didn't want to let go of what we had built together.

Deep down, I was scared to be alone. Being transgender, I didn't know if anyone else would ever want to date me.

♂

Four months later, in November 2006, we were in the bedroom folding clothes and listening to the radio. On her dresser sat a white box; inside it were matching wedding bands that we had given each other our first year together. When we separated, we had taken them off and put them in that box, where they sat and gathered dust.

"Sit down," she said.

"What? Why?" I asked as I continued to fold one of my shirts. When we worked on laundry, I stuck to folding my clothes; she hated the way I folded hers.

"Just do it," she said.

I moved to the edge of the bed and sat down. My shirt was still clasped in my hands. She moved over to the dresser and pulled down the white box. She then got down on one knee and opened the lid.

"Will you stay with me?" she asked, tears welling in her eyes.

I felt uncomfortable by the gesture of her down on one knee. My traditional values screamed that the man should be the one on a knee. I felt like she was taking away yet another aspect of my manhood that I longed to embody.

I hid my discomfort, knowing that this wasn't a proposal, and said, "Yes."

We both took our silver rings and slipped them back onto the ring fingers on our left hands. She lifted off the ground and we embraced.

It was a moment I would later describe to my coworkers, Lisa and LeeAnn, who were also my good friends. As I finished the story, I became confused by their facial expressions. Lisa sat in her office chair and kept nervously looking over toward LeeAnn, who was leaning against the desk, arms crossed.

Michelle was never an abusive partner, but they both looked at me like I was a victim of domestic violence who was announcing that I was staying with the person causing me all of the pain. I caught them looking at my ring, the light that bounced off the curved edges, and I felt like the naïve child sharing life-changing news with his skeptical parents.

My coworker LeeAnn followed me into my office and closed the door. I had confided in her for the past year about all I was going through with Michelle. She would always patiently sit and listen to my drama and then just bluntly say, "You two should break up." Bluntness was what made our friendship work.

I watched as she sat down in the chair across from my desk. She was wearing a light purple sundress, which she most likely ordered online from J.Crew. Her Thai skin looked darker in the dress. I was waiting for her to say, "What the fuck, Ryan?" But those words never came out.

"Ryan, I'm worried for you," she said. She leaned her elbows onto my desk and reached out her hands.

"Why?" I asked.

"I'm just worried that you aren't really doing what is right for you." She leaned back in her chair and tugged down on the bottom of her dress as she crossed her legs.

Her remark sent my brain to envision what was right for me. We both knew that Michelle's readiness to be committed to me again was most likely temporary, and contingent upon whether I chose to complete a surgery to change my genitalia from a vulva to a small penis and scrotum. I knew that I wanted the surgery completed, but I had surrendered the dream for our relationship.

Even with LeeAnn's concern, I continued to surrender a part of my identity until the next year when my depression surrounding my genitalia became too much for me to handle.

On August 10, 2007, I agreed to make my first appearance on *Larry King Live!* I didn't really know much about Larry's show, except that my friends, LeeAnn and Lisa, watched him and gave him the seal of approval.

It didn't fully sink in that I would be on live television and watched by millions of viewers until I stepped into the studio and felt the heat from the lamps, which surrounded the table, rest on my forehead. After starting my website and posting pictures of my transition, I began receiving offers to appear on TV, but I had always declined. All of the offers came from producers who worked for daytime-talk shows fueled by drama and heckling audience members.

When I received a phone call from producers with *Larry King Live!* I thought it was a joke, until I started talking to them. They told me they had been covering the story of a city manager in Largo, Florida, named Steve Stanton, who was fired after announcing that he was transitioning to Susan. They wanted to do a show that featured different people in the community. They mentioned that they had seen me in *Gender Rebel* and had visited my website, and so they felt I would be a nice addition to their guest panel. After I realized it wasn't a prank, I agreed to appear on Larry's show. Being on his show felt like a huge opportunity to educate the public. The fact that there wouldn't be an audience shouting catcalls was an added bonus.

My nerves kicked in when Larry looked at me as I walked up toward the chair directly across from him. His head hung lower than his shoulders, and his arms were crossed over each other as he leaned forward on the table. I wasn't sure if he'd acknowledge me, but I had hoped he would at least nod his head and say, "Hello."

"You sure don't look like a girl," his gruff voice said.

Shocked by his comment, I began to wonder if it was meant to be a compliment or if he was confused about who I was and why I was on the show.

"Well, thanks, Larry. 'Cuz I'm not," I said.

Larry then looked away from me and down at his blue sheets of paper, which contained a mixture of typed paragraphs, along with his scribbled handwriting.

"Ryan, please take a seat here," a woman said as she gestured toward a cushioned chair on rollers.

I sat down and watched as she grabbed a cord dangling from inside my suit jacket and plugged it into a black box screwed in under the table. She scooted me in and then set an earpiece in my right ear.

"You may hear people talking to you if we need something," she said.

I looked up at her as she set a black mug full of water in front of me, and then I glanced around the studio. Anything beyond the stage where we sat and the large cameras surrounding us looked like an abyss.

I knew that what I was about to do on Larry's show was going to challenge me.

The only cameras I had been in front of before were the ones used for shooting the documentary, during which I felt nurtured and had time for introspection with each question the director asked.

Now I felt alone—even with people who worked for the show running around me, and sitting shoulder to shoulder with the other guests.

"Ryan, look in camera two," I heard a voice say through my earpiece.

I swung my head back and forth before recognizing what I was instructed to do and then peered dead ahead at the camera. Peering back at me was my reflection. I kept playing with my lips to see if I could achieve an expression that didn't make me look pissed off. I failed.

A person next to one of the cameras began counting down the seconds before we would be back on the air, live.

Larry's theme music kicked on and he began to introduce me, "His name is Ryan Sallans and . . ."

It was surreal to hear Larry King say my name out loud, and I wondered if my parents were watching. I had not told them I was going on the show. It's sad to admit, but I was afraid they would be embarrassed by their child and mad at me for letting the family's secret out to those that didn't already know.

After my introduction Larry looked at me and started in with his questions.

I stuttered and stumbled; the fast pace of the show was too much for my brain to comprehend, but I tried to stay calm and articulate.

"When will you be complete?" Larry asked.

His other questions had been slightly awkward, but this one stopped all wheels from spinning in my brain.

He had just asked the question that I was struggling with the most.

I wasn't ready to answer it; and I knew that being on live TV, I didn't have time to think about what I'd really like to say. I knew I couldn't sum up a question about feeling "complete" in one sentence.

I also knew by Larry's interview style he wouldn't have the patience to listen to me explain the emotional aspect of being complete versus how one feels with being physically complete.

Knowing the sensationalism of TV, audience members would most likely associate "complete" with what was between someone's legs; so my mind wandered to how I felt about what was between mine.

I wanted to say, "When I have a penis," but I didn't want to out my desire for the surgery—on international television, no less—without first talking with Michelle.

"Well, you're never really done transitioning. So I don't know, in two to five years. . . ," I mumbled.

My response didn't make any sense, much like a lot of what I said the first time I was on his show. Probably one of the things that saved me was Larry's randomness and abrupt interruptions on most of the questions he asked.

When the show ended, I felt proud for what I had done and humbled to have been interviewed by a man who has become an icon in American broadcast history.

When I left the studio, I was invited to go out for dinner with the other guest on the show and one of the producers before the limo driver took me back to the hotel. I couldn't sleep much that night because my brain was fixated on Larry's question about feeling complete.

The educator side of me knew that being "complete" was multifaceted, but the intuitive side of me knew I needed to have the lower surgery, and I needed it soon. The biggest barrier, even beyond financing it, was my romantic relationship.

The question I had been harboring was finally on the front burner in my life: *Will Michelle leave me after I complete my final operation?*

The week after returning from Los Angeles, I repacked my bags and headed out to Seattle with Michelle. I was attending and presenting at a conference geared toward the transgender community, and I had asked Michelle if she'd like to come along so that we could make a little vacation out of the trip.

Prior to leaving, I glanced over the conference workshop schedule and noticed that a surgeon was going to be presenting his procedure and results, related to a surgery designed to create a small penis, called a metoidioplasty.

I had been researching this doctor and his work for the past three years. I had also been studying several photos that showed his outcomes. In all the photos online that I scanned through, I knew the metoidioplasty procedure would give me a very small penis, one the size of a child's. I knew the size would be a struggle for me, but it was the surgery I felt most comfortable paying for and undergoing.

I had shown pictures of the procedure to Michelle and she curled up her lips, wrinkled her nose, and said, "Gross. That looks like a puppy's penis."

Her comments hurt me, but I ended up apologizing for showing them to her. I felt guilty for wanting something else that she didn't approve of or like.

In an attempt to test the waters again with Michelle, I invited her to go to the workshop that discussed the surgical outcomes and showed photos.

The surgeon was a short man, with a large mustache, reminding me of a cartoon character from my childhood, a slender Yosemite Sam. He was dressed in a pin-striped suit and wore a bright red tie. His voice was soft and had a slight Southern drawl, even though he was located out of the Southwest.

I watched intently as he clicked on his laptop and pushed the slide show through the shots of his patients' bodies prior to surgery. I saw the torsos and bottom halves of men with all body types, sizes, and shapes.

When I looked at their genitalia, the one thing they all had in common was that their clitorises were larger and protruded slightly from their body. Testosterone causes the clitoris to change in size and shape.

"Okay, now let's look at what happened with these guys after surgery," he said while looking behind him at the projector screen.

I could tell by the way he talked about his patients that he loved his job and the patients he worked with. I sat up in my seat and allowed my periphery vision to focus on Michelle's body language.

"Here we have a photo of a patient after I finished my third stage with him, which means I just finished putting silicone implants in. I had completed his penis several months before this stage."

On the screen was an uncircumcised penis, again smaller in both length and circumference; his scrotum was sewn into two different sacs and his vaginal opening was closed completely.

I noticed Michelle stayed in the same position, and I didn't sense any tension from her body sitting next to me. The surgeon put up two more photos. I noticed when he did this, I scooted a little farther to the end of my seat and started pressing my elbows into the top of my thighs. I was more nervous than Michelle was. This was a good sign.

The crowd began to clap as he finished up his presentation. I was impressed by his work, but I didn't like that he made patients undergo several surgeries to complete the procedure. I also didn't like that the average costs for the complete procedure was over fifty thousand dollars.

As other people got up to leave, Michelle and I followed behind them.

"So what did you think?" I asked, looking down at her and studying her body language.

"It was fine. They still look funny to me."

"Huh . . ." I left it at that, too scared to hear any more.

I looked down at the conference schedule and noticed the next workshop looked at transguys and sex.

"Do you want to go to this workshop on transguys in porn with me?" I asked.

Michelle wasn't the type of person to watch porn of any kind; so I figured she would decline, but I was pleasantly surprised when she agreed.

In the workshop the facilitator showed different clips of transguys having sex. I loved watching the clips because it showed them with men and other transguys. All of the guys in the film hadn't had a lower surgery completed, so it showed some enjoying vaginal penetration while others had strapped on a dildo. I was starting to feel myself turned on by the videos, an odd feeling when you are in a room with fifty other strangers.

I began to wonder how it felt to enjoy having sex and being comfortable in your body. I still felt a great deal of shame and guilt around sex and had limited orgasms. Near the end of the workshop, Michelle leaned over toward me. I was prepared to hear her ask us to leave.

"I'm kind of horny," she whispered.

I snapped my neck and head toward her and gave her a sideways smile. I imagined the two of us having sex; her body the way it was, but mine without a vagina.

When we returned home from the conference, I felt a new wave of confidence. Having Michelle attend a transgender conference with me, where she saw other people in relationships, gave me hope that she would find more attachment to me and acceptance of others in the community. Her reaction to the workshop on transmen and sexuality finally gave me the confidence to confront her about my own body and sexuality.

When she came home from work the day after we got home, she found me sitting upstairs on our bed, staring at the ground.

"What's going on?" she asked as she sat down next to me.

"I want the metoidioplasty," I said quietly.

"I knew you did. You just had to tell me," she said without any emotional reaction.

"Really?" I asked, shocked by her response.

"Yes," she said. "I'm not sure if I can stay with you after you have it done, but I'll stay with you up until it's completed."

I was crushed by her comment, but found myself believing I didn't deserve more, since I had crushed her by transitioning. Ever since our separation, she had stated that she was with me today because she wanted to be, but she didn't know what tomorrow would bring.

My emotions felt trampled by her ambivalence to commitment and to me. I tried to push aside the hurt, but I believed I deserved to be hurt. After all, I was the one transitioning, changing my body to the gender that she didn't find attractive.

♂

That weekend I sent an e-mail to a surgeon whom I had been researching. He lived in Belgrade, Serbia, and his surgical team was gaining popularity with guys in the United States. Many of his patients had documented their experiences with the team in great detail, including photos.

As I clicked through the images and stories that the guys shared, I was more impressed by the Belgrade surgeon than I was with any surgeon in America. I also liked the fact that the surgeon, whose name was Miroslav Djordjevic, but everyone called him "Miro," completed it all in one stage, instead of requiring his patients to come back for multiple stages to complete everything. His one-stage approach and the lower costs for health care in Belgrade meant that I would spend less than twenty-five thousand dollars. I knew I didn't have the money to do it, but getting a loan for twenty-five thousand seemed a lot more doable than fifty thousand.

Within a few hours after I had sent my e-mail to him, he e-mailed me back and answered the questions I had. The next thing I knew, I had my surgery date reserved with his team for May 2008; it was seven months away. He assured me I could have the surgery earlier if I wanted, but I wanted to give Michelle time to adjust to the reality of my body changing.

It also gave me more time to try and figure out how I would come up with the money. After crunching some numbers, I realized I would have to sell fifteen houses to make the money I needed to pay for the airplane tickets, lodging, food, medication, and surgery. I knew it wouldn't be possible for me to complete that many sales, since I only sold real estate part-time and had to work my other job full-time.

While I was closing a deal for a woman who worked in banking, I inquired about loans. She was a very direct businesswoman and gave me a name and contact at a large chain. I didn't waste any time, and called them immediately and requested a loan. Due to my credit score they offered me a fifteen-thousand-dollar credit line. I quickly grabbed a pen and asked where I needed to sign to get the paperwork processed. The longer I waited to pay for the surgery, the more I knew it would cost me, since my timing was right before the recession tanked the value of the U.S. dollar and increased the value of the Euro.

When I received the call from my bank informing me that the money was in my account, I instructed them to wire two different payments, one to an account in the United States and the other to an account in Serbia. I shivered when I received the confirmation of the wire transfers, but I knew I still had to come up with more money to pay for everything outside of being in the hospital.

Through expense spreadsheets I knew I would be spending over twenty-two thousand dollars for the trip. My friend Julie suggested that I throw a party to serve as a small fund-raiser, and I agreed with this sensible game plan.

♂

Since I had thrown a party for my chest surgery and my hysterectomy, I figured it would only be appropriate to throw one where the central theme would be around penises and balls.

The headline on my party invitation read: *The One-of-a-Kind Benefit Penis Party.* The bottom declared: *Come cocked and loaded.*

Over fifty people squeezed into my house the night of the party. I asked everyone to bring dollar bills to drop into buckets stationed next to the games and bar. I wanted to keep people loose and happy, so I supplied an open bar stocked with beer, gin, vodka, tequila, and liquids used as mixers.

Michelle seemed as excited about the party as I had been. Halfway through the night I fell back in my chair when I saw her take a Jell-O shot molded into the shape of a penis and drop it into her mouth.

I felt uncomfortable by the idea of her doing that to me. It didn't look natural for her. I was scared she was doing it to appease me, so I turned my attention toward my brother, who was sharing a story with a group of people about a conversation I had with my dad when I was little.

"When Ryan was around four years old, he walked into our parents' room and around the corner into the bathroom, where our dad was standing naked."

I blushed. I remembered seeing my dad naked but not any of the other details.

"Instead of walking out, Ryan pointed to our dad's penis and asked him, 'What's that?'"

My friends began to laugh as they looked at me and shook their heads.

My brother looked at me and then said, "Our dad responded with, 'It's my penis,' and Ryan came back at him with, 'Well, I want a penis.'"

I felt my body stiffen, memories of standing out in the pastures or in my own bathroom, wishing to be like all the other guys, rushed through me.

"Our dad then pushed Ryan out of his bedroom and said, 'Yeah, well, you'll get one someday.' Little did Dad know. . . ." My brother trailed off his speech as he smiled at me.

I stood there, speechless, while everyone continued to laugh.

Just like when I was on with Larry King, I didn't tell my parents about my upcoming trip to Serbia. I didn't know how to go about explaining the procedure to them, and I felt disturbed by the idea of my parents trying to envision their kid's genitals. Most aspects of my transition were a taboo topic within my family; the details were too private and too personal to share with them.

The day before leaving for Belgrade, I counted the money raised at the party. After I took out a percentage to cover the alcohol, I was left with several hundred dollars. I knew that my parents didn't fully support or understand me, but my friends were amazing.

The sound of a door opening and closing and a plate sliding onto the nightstand next to me woke me from a lucid dream. I began to blink my eyes and focused on the blurred image of a small woman in a white dress and a stethoscope around her neck. She held in her hand a syringe, which was full of a clear fluid, and set a chart at the end of the bed by my feet.

I continued to blink in order to get my eyes to focus more clearly; I watched her move around my bed and toward the IV stand situated to the right of me.

"You eat okay?" she instructed in an accent that resembled Russian. She raised her eyebrow and pointed over to the large hunk of corn bread she had brought in.

I slowly shifted my glance over to the table next to me, one of the three pieces of furniture in my eight-by-ten room, and noticed it wasn't the American-style corn bread, which was moist and sweet. This one looked heavy, dry, and chock-full of cornmeal.

I wanted to be polite, so I nodded my head in agreement, even though the thought of food wasn't appealing to me. It was a meal and a smell I would soon have a gag reflex toward when in my presence. I had spent the past two days and nights vomiting stomach bile on the white tile floor next to my metal bed. I felt like I was in hell and dying a slow death in a hospital room halfway across the world.

The nurse ignored my disinterest in the bread and began to inspect a large bag full of fluid, which hung on the small metal hook of the IV stand. She tapped on the tubing, which ran down from the bag and attached to a large green port sticking out from the middle of my hand. She took the syringe that she had carried in and inserted the tip of its needle into a second port attached to the tube that was pushing fluid through my veins. As she began to push down on the plunger I felt a searing rush of heat followed by pain through my hand, wrist, and into the veins running through my forearm.

"All done," she said.

I whimpered as I tried to bring my heavy breathing into a regular pace.

"Okay," she said as she looked down at my catheter bag dangling from the edge of the bed on her way out of my room.

A rush of dishes clinking, women talking, and babies crying spilled over my body until the heavy door closed behind her and I was left alone, again.

The room abruptly turned silent, besides the cracking and banging of the water pipes next to my head. I was disoriented, drugged, and exhausted, but I managed to look down the length of my body to where my new genitals were healing. The only thing I could see was a tube, the diameter of a large straw, sticking out of my stomach several inches down from my belly button. How everything else looked down there was still a mystery to me. I knew by the pulsing I felt between my legs that I was swollen and most likely bruised. I had to keep my legs spread far apart. Anytime I tried to bring them together, I would feel an explosion of pain from where my new balls sat. My body was too long for the metal bed, so my legs ended up dangling over the tiny mattress.

"What did I do?" I asked.

I had never felt regret after surgery, but this time I felt different. I began to question whether it was a good idea for me not to share the news of this surgery and my trip to Belgrade, Serbia, with my parents. Tears started to drip down my face and I felt my heart increasing in pace.

"Just calm down. It will get better," I assured myself.

Michelle had kept her word and had taken two weeks off from work to join me in a foreign city and watch over me when I wasn't in the hospital. I was afraid that she wouldn't come along with me. Just two months prior to our trip, I had bought an engagement ring, asked her mom for her blessing in proposing to Michelle, and then popped the question over a candlelit dinner I had prepared.

I wanted to propose for three reasons: the first was I wanted to marry her; the second was I wanted her to have legal protections in case something happened to me in Belgrade; and the third was I was afraid of her leaving me after the operation.

But after I asked, "Will you marry me?" she looked down at the heart-shaped box that contained a titanium band holding a sapphire jewel.

With tears in her eyes Michelle replied, "No, I can't marry you now." My heart dropped from her comment, but she gave me hope when she said, "Ask me again in six months."

Her last comment echoed in my ears each day after the failed proposal.

Being awake for more than a few minutes, and happy that I had survived the operation, I began to wonder where she was, and felt angry that I was all alone. Truthfully, though, a part of me was happy she wasn't there; I was scared of her looking at my new genitals and expressing her disapproval. Tired and anxious, I felt myself dozing off again. Images and feelings associated with the few days leading up to where I was were still fresh in my mind.

The trip had not begun smoothly. What should have been an eighteen-hour trip ended up taking us twenty-six hours, due to our connecting flight in Paris deciding to leave without us on board.

I pinched myself when our final flight landed on the runway in Serbia.

As Michelle and I wheeled our bags into the small airport, we were overpowered by the strong aroma of cigarette smoke. I tried to hold my breath, already fighting a cold and not wanting the smoke to exacerbate it. After a few steps I realized it wasn't going to get much better and surrendered to the stench.

We fell into line with everyone else waiting to leave the airport security. My heart skipped beats when it was my turn to cross the yellow line and hand over my passport to the solemn uniformed man behind the glass. His eyes studied my picture and then began scanning me, searching for anything that didn't match.

After a few minutes he stamped a page and slid the passport back under the window. I waited for Michelle to pass through, and then stepped past security into the crowd that was anxiously awaiting their loved ones' arrivals.

I scanned the crowd, and on my second pass I was able to hone in on a white piece of paper with the name *Sallans* scribbled on it. I followed the hands holding the paper upward and noticed a tall, broad-shouldered man with dark facial features, a small nose, and eyes that reminded me of Elvis Presley's. They were dark, with long lashes, and spaced farther apart than normal. I walked up to him and motioned for Michelle to follow me. Her face had her recognizable checked-out and annoyed expression, which I tried to ignore, and reminded myself that she was just as exhausted as I was.

"You Ryan?" he asked.

"Yes," I said. I was happy to see that they had got my frantic e-mail from the Paris airport with the new flight plan listed.

"Welcome, my name is Marko," he said before shaking my hand and then Michelle's. "You Americans always travel so light," he joked as he grabbed the handles to our bags and led us outside to his car. It was nice to get out of the airport and into fresh air, but immediately I noticed the distinct smell of Belgrade. It reminded me of a mixture of diesel and asphalt on a hot summer day.

Michelle and I had been up for over a day at this point, but we still had to meet the main surgeon, Dr. Miro, before we could retire for the evening. I loved that even his staff called him by the nickname Miro. I did it because I couldn't pronounce his last name, but I felt like the staff did it because they all worked as a team. Status and hierarchy didn't seem important to them, which was another reason I liked them. I tried to take in the landscapes around me as we drove away from the airport and into the city, but it was too dark to make out anything but the lights running up and down the buildings.

Marko's small Honda wove through the streets' intersections. His driving made me very nervous, and I found myself being the passenger driver pushing my foot on the imaginary brake I wished had existed on my side of the car.

When he pulled up onto a sidewalk outside a four-story brick building, I was happy to find us still alive. I had never met Dr. Miro. My only contact with him had been through e-mail, so I was curious to meet him in person. The apartment door swung open to expose a man about the same height as me, with brown hair and a face bearing a striking resemblance to Rowan Atkinson's TV show character, Mr. Bean. His face was long, a sign of the daily stress he underwent as a surgeon. He had bushy eyebrows, small brown eyes, a prominent nose, and small lips, which were always smiling.

"Ryan! Welcome!" Dr. Miro said as he extended his arms for a hug. "Come in, come in," he said as he motioned for us to enter into his small apartment and over to his couches. Before my butt even hit the leather-covered cushion, he quickly began to go over the details of the surgery and who would be contacting me. He spoke fast, like he had just slammed down a full pot of coffee.

If I wasn't so exhausted, I would have probably spoken at the same pace due to excitement.

"Do you want to see your testicles?" he asked.

"Yes, that would be great," I said while glancing over to Michelle.

Her hands were clasped as she leaned forward and rested her elbows on her thighs. I didn't feel very settled seeing her move into that position—the position I referred to as her "tough" pose. I kept looking at her so that I could try to gauge her reaction to the idea of me having a scrotum. She had said several times in the past that she didn't like penises and hated balls. Her disdain made me scared to share this experience with her.

"Here you go," Dr. Miro said as he came around the corner with shrink-wrapped plastic bags. Inside of them were two egg-shaped objects about the size of chocolate Cadbury eggs. "Squeeze them," he instructed. "They are very natural. Very nice . . ."

My fingers gently wrapped around both sides and squeezed. I was scared of rupturing them, but I realized very quickly they would stand up to the pressure.

Miro was pleased with my squeezing and laid the bags on his coffee table. "Good, yes?"

I nodded my head in response and wondered what was going through Michelle's mind as she sat there watching all of this unfold in front of her.

"I give you lifetime guarantee on them. . . . You even get a card saying this," he said, proud of the quality of implants that he used. "I will even upgrade the size of them in the future. You just tell me."

"Uh, okay." I laughed. "But I think these will be good enough."

"Okay, my friend," he said. "Marko will take you to the apartment. You rest and enjoy tomorrow. I will see you in two days for surgery."

I knew that I was lacking sleep, which made me question if everything happening on this trip was all a dream. I pinched myself as we pulled up to the apartment that would be our home for the next fourteen days. The one thing I never thought I'd ever get to complete—the lower surgery—was finally happening.

When I first started my transition, I was one of the guys who said, "I don't need the lower surgery. It's not what's between the legs that counts, and no one sees that part of me, anyway."

Which, of course, is true. It's not what's between the legs that counts. But I knew deep down when I said that, I wasn't trying to be politically correct. It was because I believed I'd never be able to afford the surgery. So what was the point in dreaming about it?

After meeting Miro and touching the samples, which represented what would be my new balls, I knew that all of my hard work and financial planning were paying off.

The next morning Michelle and I stepped out into a world where we quickly realized we didn't belong. I'm used to feeling like an outsider and not belonging in a community, but being overseas in a city and culture completely different from my own was very stressful. Besides walking through some neighborhoods and looking at various houses, we kept to ourselves and stayed in the apartment.

The morning of my operation, I woke up and began to follow the instructions given to me by Miro. First on the list was to shave my pubic area, including abdomen and butt cheeks. I quickly learned that this isn't easy to do when you can't see where you're shaving. I also realized the best way to go was to skip the shaving cream and just run the razor over my body while my parts were underwater.

After I was satisfied with the amount of body hair that I had shaved off, I left the bathroom and wound down the wooden stairs to the first floor. On the first level of the apartment sat a balcony that overlooked a pink building and its backyard, which was lined with pine trees. I went out with the one glass of water I was allowed to drink and took in my surroundings. Michelle soon came out to join me. We sat there like an old couple and listened to the children playing soccer below us while we breathed in the warm May air.

Around noon a doctor we hadn't met yet came to pick us up. When I answered the door to see who it was, my gaze went up from his long legs, to his fanny pack wrapped around his waist, and settled on his dark hair framing his smooth facial features. Michelle and I both agreed that a majority of the young Serbian men were very good-looking.

He introduced himself and then grabbed my hospital bag and escorted us to his car. Riding in a car during the daytime allowed me to take in and study the city composed of multistoried buildings nestled among the hills and between the trees that stretched for miles. I felt more comfortable with this doctor's driving, but I didn't feel comfortable being on the small, winding streets and around other cars filled with drivers who didn't believe in using turn signals or following a speed limit. Driving in Belgrade would never be an option for me. It felt more like a game of bumper cars than organized driving.

As we entered into the heart of the city, the doctor took a sharp turn and drove us through a parking garage. The parking spots were a lot smaller than what I was used to seeing in the States. I assumed they didn't need as much space since SUVs were almost nonexistent there. Most of the vehicles were manual-transmission four-door sedans.

As we emerged from the parking garage and began walking down the sidewalk, the doctor said, "We are now in Old Belgrade. The city is divided by the river, so on the other side is where all of the newer buildings and companies are located."

I looked around and felt a feeling of despair rush over me. A majority of the buildings were composed of crumbling brick, stone, and mortar held together by the spray-painted graffiti. The storefronts resembled a toothless smile; the windows had been knocked out either by vandals or by the repercussion of bombs dropped by NATO in the nineties.

The doctor pointed to the hospital, one of the taller and more stable buildings on the tight block, and then pointed back toward the garage so Michelle would have a feel for the main street. After I was checked into the hospital, she would be going solo. I couldn't imagine having to navigate the city and the bus system on my own, but she seemed okay with it.

At this point her balls were bigger than mine!

As we neared the hospital entrance, we were stopped by a guard. No one got by without checking in with him. The floors were marble, and the walls were stained yellow from the cigarette smoke. We were led up a dark stairwell. The old stairs were chipped and the wood banister was missing most of its varnish from all the hands that had grasped it over the years. After four flights we arrived on the floor where I would spend the next four days. We slipped green booties over our shoes before walking past the stainless-steel doors and into a bright hallway.

When we passed through the doors, I felt as if we had just emerged from a world where no one else existed. Here, life was bustling again, with nurses walking quickly back and forth between rooms, holding trays of food and bags full of fluids. The doctor escorted me to my private room.

When we entered, I felt like I was in another world again; things were quiet and calm. The walls were white, since smoking wasn't allowed past the first floor, and the room was bland. There were no machines or technology there. The most technology they had was the TV that sat at the foot of the bed.

A small brown-haired nurse showed me to the old metal-framed bed.

"Lay here," she said while patting the mattress.

She was one of the three nurses who could speak some English. I could tell they were embarrassed to speak in front of me, but I appreciated their effort. The only word I was really focused on saying to them was *"boli,"* pronounced "bowl-e," which means "pain."

"This will hurt, a little," the nurse said as she searched for a vein on my hand to put in one of three IVs.

I cringed as I felt the needle running up my vein; it inserted a tiny tube that ran two inches inside my body. I heard a small knock on the door and looked over to see Miro entering the room. He was still in blue jeans, sandals, and a black T-shirt.

"Hello, my friend," he said as he found a chair to sit in. He threw his right leg over his left knee, scooted down in the chair, and put his arms behind his head. "How are things today?"

"Good," I said. My heart was beating at a slightly faster pace, but not as much as I would have expected. This would be my third surgery in three years; it was becoming a routine.

"Look at you, sitting there so calm." He laughed.

"I'm used to this by now," I said.

"So the surgery will take about four or five hours; then we wheel you back here for recovery. Do you have any questions?"

"No." I was always bad at asking questions. Plus we had covered the details after I had arrived two nights prior.

"Okay, then, we start soon." He got up and headed out the door. The other doctor who had brought us to the hospital asked Michelle to go with him, leaving me alone with the nurses.

A young nurse stuck her head through the doorway. "Hello," she said.

She had a smaller voice, not as assertive in tone as the others. She was younger, and had freckled cheeks and long red hair, which was pulled back into a bun. I instantly liked her. She reminded me of Megan, my childhood friend.

"So go ahead and put this on. Everything else must go off," she said as she extended a folded gown toward me.

I took it from her and let it unfold. It had a small stain on the front that couldn't be anything else but blood. I shrugged off the difference in quality of medical supplies and hygiene expectations here versus back home. I tried to make myself feel better by saying they just recycle. After I got the gown on, I sat back on the bed, hiding my bare butt from all of the nurses. Later I would learn my modesty was unnecessary, since I was naked most of the time I was there.

The door swung open again by the force of a squeaky metal gurney. Two nurses were pushing it into the room.

"Get on," the cute nurse instructed me as she patted the hard metal surface.

Still holding the backs together, I walked toward the gurney while they wheeled the metal stand holding the IV bag behind me. After my body was fully extended on the gurney, they began pushing and pulling on the cart, but the wheels weren't cooperating, so it took another nurse to get it straightened out and rolling down the hallway. I watched the ceiling pass by as I listened to them speak Serbian. I wondered what they were talking about. I feared that they were making fun of me and my awkward-fitting gown, but I pushed the fear away. From what I had read and seen, professionals in European countries were more open and accepting of transgender individuals.

We rode on an old elevator down one floor. From the noises the elevator was making, and the amount of time it took to move just one floor, I suspected it wouldn't pass U.S. safety codes. The old metal doors slowly rolled open to a secluded hallway. We wheeled past a security guard, who was sitting stoically by the doors of the dim-lit operating theater.

Like any other operating room, its temperature was about ten degrees cooler than the rest of the rooms. I started to shiver. The coolness rushed over my legs and up the opening of the gown. I glanced around the room for warm blankets, like the ones that had been draped over my body in previous surgeries. There weren't any in sight.

Several people lifted me to the operating table and then instructed me to put my lower legs up on some cold metal stirrups. It took me a second to realize they were motioning for me to scoot my butt toward them. I kept scooting and they kept motioning until my legs were perpendicular to my torso. My nerves began to kick in and my face started to flush with red.

The gown no longer covered the lower half of my body; my genitals and butt were completely exposed to everyone in the room. The way the operating bed was positioned, I was facing the swinging doors and the security guard. I wondered how many times in this hospital the guards had seen men like me—guys who had strong builds, strong features, and a vulva.

I wanted to ask them to cover me up, but I couldn't find my voice. Instead, I found fear overcoming me. A nurse must have sensed my discomfort and draped a small towel over my genitals, soon to be splayed like a frog in a science classroom.

"Okay, Ryan," my anesthesiologist's voice ran over me. "Take some deep breaths for me."

He placed a large plastic cup over my face and I began taking in what I thought was oxygen. The next thing I knew, I woke up to several people around me, all motioning toward my body. I felt like I had just emerged from the dark surroundings of a lake that had a thick layer of ice over the surface. My body shivered as my breath fought to find a rhythm. Nurses ran to grab blankets and started to layer them on top of my body.

I was in hypothermic shock.

"What's wrong?" the doctor asked.

"My . . . my—my ca-ca-calves," I responded, shivering.

"What's wrong with your calves?"

"They hurt!" I said, confused by what had just happened.

The shivering was bad, but the pain radiating through the core of my calves, down to my ankles and back up to my knees, was worse. Assistants to the doctors slowly lifted my legs up and began pumping my feet like I was pushing on the accelerator in a car.

"Is that helping?" he asked.

"Not really," I said, but my shivers started to lessen.

"Hmm, that's strange. It must be because you have large calf muscles."

A part of me felt proud of my body and the size of my calf muscles, which came from my genetics and all the cycling and running that I did in preparation for the surgery. The other part of me wished I hadn't worked so hard because, I believed, if my muscles were smaller, then I wouldn't have been in so much pain.

They began to wheel me out of the cold room, back toward my private bed and space. The vomiting began a few hours after the operation. I first leaned over and puked on the pink sheet they had draped over my shoulder, in case I had to puke. After a couple times of using the sheets, I surrendered to leaning over the bed and letting it out on the floor.

I felt horrible for the night nurses. Each time I puked, they would change the sheets with me in the bed, change my shirts, and mop the floor. I was not an easy patient.

The doctors found a reason for my illness after drawing labs the second day.

♂

The ringing of the phone shot me out of my sleep. I was still alone in the hospital room—no sign of Michelle.

I reached over for the phone and answered, "Hello?"

"Hello, Ryan." The voice was deep and serious. It was the voice of the doctor who had administered my anesthesia.

"Hey. . . ," I replied.

"How are you feeling?"

"Uh, not good," I said as I looked down at my shirtless body. After puking on three gowns, they quit wasting their time.

"Okay, well, bad news. You can't leave today. Your liver enzymes are too high, which is why you are probably not able to keep anything down. The head of the hospital wants you to stay two more days."

I felt tears well up in my eyes. I didn't want to be there any longer. I wanted to get away from the banging pipes, the crying babies, the smell of corn bread, the endless shots that caused one of my veins to explode, and the feeling of being forgotten.

"Okay. . . ," I agreed, knowing that I wasn't in any shape to leave the hospital. And even if I was, I couldn't do anything about it.

At this moment Michelle opened the door and poked her head in. She had been wandering around the city on her own after having problems getting past security at the entrance of the hospital. She seemed happy to see that I was awake; the past two days when she had sat by my side, I was dead to the world.

I hung up the phone and looked at her. I was relieved to have her with me, even though I was still terrified of her seeing my body.

This fear was heightened that night when Marko came to visit and to change my bandages. Michelle had spent the whole day with me watching the Animal Planet channel on TV. It was nice to be able to stay awake for longer than a few minutes at a time.

"Hello, how you feeling?" Marko asked as he walked in. In his hands were a motorcycle helmet and a brown paper bag.

"Better. I haven't puked the whole day."

"Good, that means the new drugs are working." He set his helmet down on the chair and reached into the bag. "I brought you some good homemade chicken and carrots. Get you something different than this hospital food." He set the meal down on the side table. I could smell the chicken and also picked up on potatoes. I knew I couldn't eat right then, but I was extremely excited to try it later.

"So," he said as he clapped his hands and rubbed them against each other. "You ready to see your penis?"

My heart stopped for a second. Three days and I still hadn't looked at it. I had gotten up out of bed to move around slowly, like a penguin, and to try and use the bathroom for things other than urinating. Still, I hadn't looked down.

I was scared, but also very curious.

"Of course!" I said.

"Okay, then." He put on a pair of latex gloves and laid a pair of scissors and new gauze on the bed. "Michelle, you can grab a camera and take some pictures, if you like."

"Okay," she said, compliant.

I looked at her with fear. I wanted to tell her she didn't have to take any pictures if she didn't want to, but I decided she could judge her comfort on her own.

His fingers gently pulled on the medical tape that was around my new penis and scrotum. He lifted the tape off and the gauze that was soaked completely through with blood. I peeked over my bloated belly. It was finally settling in that the parts of my body that had caused me so much dysphoria were finally replaced.

"This is looking very good," he said as he lifted the gauze off and showed me my penis.

It was swollen, red, stitched up, and bloody, but it was mine. Even though it was only about two inches in length, I was happy to see something that looked more male. Marko grabbed a mirror and showed me my scrotum. At this point it was swollen and bruised, appearing like two mangos instead of the normal size of kiwis.

"The swelling will continue to go down, and in a couple of months, you'll be good as new," he said with confidence.

Looking at my body, I knew that the healing from this surgery would require a lot more patience than any other procedure I had ever undergone.

Soft voices, too quiet to make out what was being said, ran up the vents and into the bathroom where I stood. Michelle was downstairs, watching TV, and I was finishing up with my bath after a six-mile run. The cool front leading into the fall weather was starting to make running outside more pleasant after all the hot and humid heat of Nebraska's summer.

I was six months into the healing process—no more mango-size balls, swollen penis tissue, tubes jutting from my abdomen, or infections.

I was still adjusting to running with my new balls in place. I noticed that my gait, even when walking, was wider. My close friends kept asking, "When are you going to stop walking like a cowboy who's just gotten off his horse?"

I laughed with them, even though I felt slightly insecure by the attention given to me and the fascination my friends seemed to have toward my genitals.

Cool droplets of water fell from the side of my cheeks, ran down my chest, and slowly scooted along the contours of my leg. My clothes were bundled up on the floor next to me. I found myself standing in front of the mirror, which hung above our sink, and fighting the urge to cover my body up with a towel, like I usually did after getting out of the bath. With all of the time and money I put into my body, I was forcing myself to look at it in its true form—no clothing or towels to hide behind.

My reflection cast an image I still struggled to embrace fully, an image I tried not to dissect and judge. I tried to appreciate my form by focusing on what I liked about my body. My thick sideburns, my prominent brow and jawline, and my green eyes were all satisfying to me. I took pride in my shoulders and torso, which would never be seen as female. My stomach lacked defined abs, but there wasn't an overabundance of fat covering them, either.

I felt my blood pressure increase when I started to head farther south and took in my hips, butt, and thighs. Small love handles curved out and led down to saddlebags, which wouldn't go away—no matter how much I worked out. During high school and college, all of my boyfriends would comment on my butt and how they liked its round shape. I didn't like it then, and now whenever I looked in the mirror, the round shape screamed "female" to me. I know I should embrace my round butt—it gives me more cushion when I'm sitting down and it helps hold my jeans up—but I hate it.

I closed my eyes and shook my head in an attempt to jumble the female image I had in my mind when looking at my lower half. I reopened them and allowed myself to take in the whole picture: a broad-shouldered man with curves and a small penis, with average-size balls hanging behind it, the right one sat higher than the left.

The surgeons made my penis by releasing my clitoris from the ligaments that held it in place and wrapping my labia minora tissue around it to create a shaft. They used my inner cheek tissue to create a urethral extension, which runs through the penis like any man's, and attaches to my old urethra. This allows me to pee standing up and through the fly of my pants, if I choose. My surgeons then closed off the vaginal opening and used my labia majora tissue as the scrotum, which houses my silicone implants.

To have a "full-size" penis, I could have chosen the procedure that took a large skin graft from my body and required several surgeries over a year, but the thought of the money and the amount of time didn't appeal to me. I have what many guys are seeking: genitals that resemble that of a man's, even if they are small.

Now, my biggest challenge was to embrace my penis fully, even if it didn't measure up.

With each month of recovery, it was hard for me not to reach down and touch myself when I was alone. So I reached my right hand down and let my fingers slowly start to rub on the shaft. It took over four months to be able to touch it without a searing pain. Now when I touched it, I could feel blood rush through the tissue, and then watched as it slowly grew and extended away from my body. It only grew to two inches—a size people love to make jokes about—but it was my natural tissue and formed a natural erection from arousal and stimulation.

My mind was deep in a fantasy of me being touched by a stranger, but it was interrupted by the urge to pee. I stepped over to the toilet and lifted both the seat and the lid. I didn't have any clothes on, so I just stood in front of the bowl and tried to relax. It was still an adjustment for me to relax enough to pee standing up; but with each month that passed, I was getting better at letting it go and dealing with the mess afterward.

After a few seconds I started to feel a stream leaving my urethra. I was amazed to see that it was following a solid stream instead of just spraying like a hose nozzle set on mist. My doctors explained that it would take time for the urethra to heal, and for my body to find the right pressure. Six months appeared to be the magic number for me. I searched the linoleum floor for any puddles, but there weren't any. This was the first day I didn't need to wipe down and disinfect the floor. I looked over everything one more time before flushing, and then stood up as tall as my body could take me under the slanted ceilings.

"I am fully potty trained," I said, smiling with the realization that I could now go into public restrooms without worrying about my bladder pressure.

My smile became even wider when I realized this opened up the possibility of me using urinals instead of another dirty stall. I walked back over to the mirror to look at myself one more time. I imagined standing in front of a lover with my nude body, having them give me a blow job while my back leaned against a wall, and then being able to penetrate them the way I had always fantasized. My hips were made for the motions, but I didn't feel comfortable with Michelle; and I knew my penis could rub against, but not fully penetrate, a woman.

I grabbed my boxers and T-shirt and slid into the bedroom, where I could spend some more time alone. I enjoyed my fantasies and exploring my body. My imagination wandered toward images of me having sex with other men. Ever since I had had my surgery, I noticed that I was more curious about how my body would respond to another man's. I knew that if I wanted to, I could have a guy in bed in a heartbeat. Ever since my transition I had become a hot commodity in the gay community and online.

I resisted the urge to go out on the prowl, and instead played out fantasies in my mind where I was with other people, both men and women. I knew how I felt when Michelle was playing with the idea of leaving me, and I felt I couldn't do the same to her.

Although Michelle had said she wasn't sure if she could stay with me after the surgery, things seemed to be going well. In fact, she expressed how she felt more comfortable with me since we had returned from Belgrade. I knew it took a lot of courage for her to express her comfort with me. Saying it out loud suggested that she wasn't just a lesbian, but could also be romantically attracted to and in love with a man.

I had hoped that after the surgery I would feel more confident being in my skin around her. That didn't happen. After we would have sex, I found myself falling into the same habits I had before the surgery: quickly slipping out of bed and putting on my clothes so that she wouldn't see me. No matter what I did to change the skin I was in, I couldn't find genuine peace with her.

The times when I did feel peace were when I was working or out at the bars with my friends. Through the years I've noticed that the biggest change in my personality after my transition was my need and desire to be around people. I had a large group of friends, from all backgrounds, that were always up for hanging out. Each time I started to feel myself slip into an uncomfortable space at home, I would text a group of my friends and end up inviting them over to watch a movie, or we would go out to one of the local dive bars, which became our second and third homes.

I wasn't a big drinker before my transition, but with my increased desire to be around people also came an increased desire for beer. After several hangovers I knew I was using alcohol to cope with my anxiousness and depression related to my job and relationship. However, even with this awareness, I wouldn't stop. Part of my identity had become being the friend who would always be up for going out drinking. I became the happy drunk who gave good hugs, instead of Ryan, the transgender advocate.

The nights that I spent at home, I didn't drink more than a couple of beers before switching to hot tea and water as Michelle and I watched our television series. Our interests in the same TV programs were one of the only things left that we had in common. When we first started dating, we always sat next to each other on the couch. Now I sat in my recliner and she sat on the couch with our two large dogs.

On the weekends one or both of us would end up at the office to do paperwork or wander out to a home improvement store for supplies to finish another home project. We had reached what our lesbian friends referred to as "lesbian bed death."

Not being a lesbian, I just called it "bed death." Having no desire for sex with my partner bothered me, especially since I was only a thirty-year-old man with high testosterone levels running through my body. The troubles I had were pushed aside when death outside of my bedroom soon followed.

Standing behind my older brother, Greg.

My phone vibrated in my pocket as I walked through the canned-goods aisle in an overcrowded grocery store. I pulled the phone out and saw my brother's name pop up. Most of our conversations took place over text messaging, so I hesitated before answering.

"What's up?" I asked.

"Grandma died this morning," his emotionless voice replied.

"Oh, no," I said. I stopped in front of the corn and stood there, leaning against the shopping cart.

♂

My kind and sweet grandma, who resembled in both looks and spirit a dark-haired Betty White, was gone. She was the person who taught me how to tie my shoes after all of the failed attempts I had in preschool. She also taught me how to blow bubbles with bubble gum, make vacuum noises through a straw after finishing a root-beer float, and sing the old folk song "Schnitzelbank" in German. When I was little, she would always grab my bare feet and start wiggling my toes as she went through all of the little piggies.

As I got older, she would share stories of growing up on a farm in Kansas, before going to business college, where she worked toward a degree as a secretary. Before finishing school, she moved to Washington, D.C., to be a clerk and typist in the War Department. I loved the story of how she and my grandpa, who served in the military during World War II, met.

While living in Washington, D.C., she was dragged to a USO dance by one of her roommates at the boarding house she was living in. As she stood at the dance, feeling out of place around all of the soldiers and other girls, she noticed a young man with strong facial features and hair styled like a Hollywood heartthrob walking around all the ladies. As she watched him, she thought to herself, *I wish he would ask me to dance.* Her heart fluttered as she watched him start to walk up to her, but her excitement stopped when he grabbed another girl to take onto the dance floor. He did this two more times, before walking up to her and saying, "Okay, let's dance."

They ended up being dance partners the rest of the night. When they started dancing together, he asked, "What's your name?"

She replied, "LaVerna."

"I like it," he said. By the end of the night he asked, "What's your last name?"

"Grafel," she said.

"I don't like it," he said. "I am going to have to change it. . . . I only have ten cents in my pocket. May I buy you a Coke?"

After that night my grandma knew she wasn't interested in her boyfriend any longer. She began dating and then married my grandpa Ralph.

After hearing her stories, I knew where my Dad got some of his romantic side, even though I don't remember my grandpa. When I was two years old, he died from congestive heart failure after battling emphysema due to heavy smoking. I have heard great stories about him, but also stories of him physically and emotionally abusing my dad when he was growing up.

Sometimes when I look at my dad, I can see the pain he carries from the memories he has of my grandpa. I hate seeing my dad in pain; he has so many emotions to express, but I can tell he holds back due to how his father treated him and what his father taught him *a man* should be.

Unlike the pain that my grandpa caused, my grandma's enduring legacy was her laugh, her kindhearted spirit, and her love, which was infectious.

♂

My emotions became bipolar with the news of her death. A part of me felt sadness, and the other part felt relief. She was diagnosed with moderate Alzheimer's on the same day I had completed my chest surgery. For her to spend the last few years of her life living in fear, forgetfulness, and sorrow was heart-wrenching for me to consider. She deserved happiness until the end.

While on the phone with my brother, I expressed my conflicted feelings. "I know. . . ," he said, pausing, ". . . but it's a good thing."

"It still sucks," I said.

"Yeah . . . it does. I left a message with Mom and Dad. Their phones are off. I'm guessing they'll call us all sometime tonight."

Since their retirement, my parents began traveling down to Florida every year to work at Disney World. It gave them something to do in a climate more forgiving than Nebraska's. It also was a way for them to escape the reality of life and the hardships that fragmented us. How can one feel sad when you are at the most magical place on earth?

"Okay, talk to you later. . . . I love you," I said as I heard his end click.

I knew my brother was right. Losing her was horrible, but having her suffering finally come to an end was a good thing. Over the past year, she didn't know who anyone was, including herself. She had spent the year sitting in her chair at the nursing home and crying because she felt so alone. "No one comes to visit me," she would sob, even when my parents or sister were sitting right in front of her.

If I had been the only one in her life, she would have been right. I never made a trip to my hometown to visit her the last year of her life. Although my dad had at first said I could never see her again—after managing with his own anger and sorrow around my transition—he took that statement back.

For the first few years of my transition, I did see her. However, I was afraid that with each year that passed, the more dramatically my appearance and voice changed, the more confused she would be around me. I was also afraid of feeling anger and frustration around her for not remembering anything about her family, and for not being able to be there for me anymore. I realized my actions were partly selfish and became ashamed.

Alzheimer's is unfair.

Michelle walked up to me as I dropped the phone to my side. She could tell something was wrong by the look on my face.

"Are you okay?" she asked.

"My grandma died today," I said.

"Oh, I'm sorry," she said, placing her hand on my upper arm. "Do we need to go home?"

"No." I started pushing the cart and moving on to our next item on the grocery list: *peanut butter, Skippy's Natural.* "It's okay."

I wasn't really okay. Ever since I began my transition, one of my biggest fears was that my parents wouldn't want me at my grandma's funeral, due to the potential shame and embarrassment of my transition. Most of my grandma's relatives are farmers or blue-collar workers who live in western Kansas. I figured transsexuality was a topic my parents didn't really want to address with them.

When Michelle and I returned home from the grocery store, I helped her bring all of the yellow plastic bags inside, and then I excused myself and retreated upstairs to our bedroom. My heart pounded in my chest as I held down the speed dial button that directed me to my parents' cell phone.

"Hi, you've reached . . ." Their phone wasn't on, only voice mail.

"Hey, Mom and Dad, I got the call from Greg. Call me tonight or tomorrow if you'd like to talk," I said. I hung up my phone and fell back onto the mattress, arms extended out on either side.

As I lay there, I tried to make myself cry, but I couldn't. One of the most frustrating things about testosterone is the inability to cry. Some people say that testosterone makes your tear ducts smaller, which makes it harder for tears to pass through. I believed this statement because before I transitioned it was physically easy for me to cry; now, even with all of the hurt and I pain that I had gone through, the tears always seemed to get stuck.

A half hour later my phone rang. I looked at the caller ID: *Dad.* When I answered, I heard my mom's voice. She explained to me what the plans were, and asked if I could make it to the funeral that Thursday.

I didn't respond right away. I was still in shock that they wanted me there, in our hometown, and in public.

I responded by saying, "Sure, if you want me to be there."

"Of course, we do," she said.

I hung up the phone, still in disbelief.

A half hour later my phone rang again. I looked at the caller ID: *Dad,* again.

Perhaps they changed their mind, I thought as I answered, expecting to hear my mom's voice.

"Hello," I said.

"Hey, Ryan." It was my dad's voice. "I was just talking with your brother and wanted to know if you'd be willing to be a pallbearer at the funeral."

"Of course, if you want me to," I said.

I began to question myself, and if his request was something real or just made up in my mind.

"Okay, as far as what to wear, we're all wearing suits, so I don't know . . ." His voice trailed off.

"That's fine. I have one I can wear, too."

"Okay, see you Thursday," he said before hanging up.

My dad's request made me feel as if everything I had gone through those past few years was worth it because now I had my family back. I was still worried about being there, in front of family members I didn't really know, and townsfolk who knew me from my past. I kept having images of them looking at me, then turning to each other, pointing and laughing. I feared that my presence would make the whole room uneasy, and that my family would be embarrassed by their transgender child.

The day of the funeral couldn't have arrived soon enough. I just wanted it to be over so that I could assess what damage I did.

We pulled up outside the funeral home. It was a gray ranch-style building that could have been disguised as just a regular home sitting in the small neighborhood. The only thing that made it resemble something other than a home was the large paved parking lot, which used to be a backyard.

I noticed my dad's white pickup was one of the only cars in the lot. The family was asked by the funeral director to arrive a half hour before the room was open to the public. My parents wanted us to arrive early so that our family could have some time together. I was relieved to see my brother pull up beside me; my niece and nephew were also in the car. My nephew, Drew, pressed his face against the glass. His nose looked flat as he made a goofy face and waved at me. I waved back, even though I already felt exhausted by his endless energy.

Seeing my hand drop back down, Drew tried to open the back door, still locked. I could see his mouth moving, ordering my brother to unlock it. I heard a click and then saw him jump out of the backseat, a couple of plastic cars followed him. He left these on the ground and slammed the car door before bolting toward me.

"Why is it always so cold and cloudy on days there are funerals?" he asked. His voice was still high-pitched in his nine-year-old body.

"I don't know," I said as I gave him a hug.

My heart was pounding in my chest and my thoughts weren't very clear, partly because of my grandma's death, but mostly because I was going to be around relatives whom I hadn't seen in at least a decade. I would be presenting to them as Ryan.

My parents had never seen me in a suit before, and I wasn't sure how they would react. I buttoned the top button of my suit coat and tugged on the bottom to help with any wrinkles from the drive as I walked up the wooden ramp and to the metal door.

I drew a deep breath in before pushing the door open and stepping foot into a room filled with somber heaviness. The scene before me felt like a movie. My mom, my sister, and her small daughter all stood together, arms around each other, while their bodies heaved up and down from crying.

My dad rounded the corner. His walk was quickly paced and authoritative. In his hands were two framed pictures of my grandma. One was from when she was a rosy-cheeked toddler; the other was a posed picture of her, before her health started to fail, for the church directory. When my dad and I made eye contact, I felt my spine straighten and my chest puff out. I wanted to look tall and strong for him. He set the photos down by the guestbook before coming over and giving me a hug.

We didn't talk. We just hugged, before he turned around to take care of more business.

I looked over my right shoulder and noticed all of my relatives whom I hadn't seen in over fifteen years. I decided to avoid them for the moment and go over to console my mom and sister.

My mom's face looked worn and thin. The stress of my grandma's failing health had taken a toll on both of my parents' bodies.

"Hey," she said as I hugged her.

"Hey, Mom."

"Just so you know, we haven't told any of the other family members about you," she said as she nodded her head toward her right.

"Okay," I said.

I crossed my arms over my chest and stood taller. I wondered if I should even act like a family member or just an overly supportive friend.

"We just figured with everything, it wasn't the right time to talk about it." She wiped her nose with her crumpled tissue before sniffing.

"No problem . . . I understand."

I didn't want the day to be about me, and I didn't really see myself being a part of my extended family's lives after that day. I scooted farther away from my mom.

My uncle, a man who hadn't spoken with me for the past seven years because my sexuality didn't fit into his traditional values, walked up to me. He's a heavyset man, someone who had struggled with his weight his whole life. It was strange to see that his black hair was now mostly gray and that his face carried more wrinkles than what were in my memory.

"Wait a second . . . just wait," he said jokingly. He always tried to make jokes in awkward situations. Typically, his comedy routines were about his weight and food. "Something is different," he said as he placed his hand on my shoulder and started to shift my body from side to side. I stood there, nervously laughed, and just went with his shtick, ignoring the fact that he had ignored me for the majority of my adult life.

"Is it your hair? Hmm, I don't know," he said before leaning down to hug me. "No matter what you look like, you're family, you're blood, and I love you," he said before kissing me on the cheek.

"Thanks, Dale," I said. A part of me was happy to hear those words and wondered if I would see him again. The other part of me felt it was his way to make peace for past words said, but that we wouldn't have a relationship in the future. This wouldn't be his fault. We lived in different worlds and had different views, but what we had in common was the same avoidant personality—it ran in our family. My uncle walked away just as my grandma's family began walking over to where I stood. I didn't have much connection, but I knew my dad was very close to them and all of their stories.

This is it, I thought.

They all recognized Greg, but they kept looking at me with confusion on their faces. My grandma's sister, who stood five-four and had the same type of hairstyle as my grandma's—short with a perm, strands of grays mixed with black—was the first to approach me.

"Now, who are you?" her meek voice asked.

I knew then I could have pulled off just being the guy in the back whom no one knew if I had arrived with the *non*family people.

"I'm Ryan," I said.

"Oh," she said as she nodded her head. I could tell she was trying to process my name and appearance. "How are you related?"

"I'm this guy's brother," I said as I reached out and hit my brother's arm. My mind was spinning and I could feel sweat starting to sweep from under my arms.

"Oh." She nodded again, bewildered as hell. She looked like she was trying to solve a math equation in her head as her eyes darted back and forth between Greg and me. I knew she wanted to say, "You can't be his brother. Paul and Joyce only have one son."

I felt embarrassed and panicked. I didn't want to explain who I was any further and be blamed for causing a scene at my grandma's funeral, so I blurted out, "It's a long story, just go with it."

I quickly leaned down and hugged her, still in disbelief at how unsmooth I felt in that room. I could feel her body tense up and heard a nervous "Oh" escape her lungs.

As I released the world's most awkward hug, I saw her husband limp up behind her. He looked at me and then looked over toward my dad, who had just joined our little circle. I hadn't had a chance to talk with my dad before this. I started to feel the sweat roll down the small of my back from my nerves. The old man smiled as he reached his frail hand out to shake my dad's.

Then my dad said what I had been waiting five years to hear.

"This is my son Ryan."

I looked at him and felt his right hand rest on my left shoulder. I was stunned, but also proud of him. He had just started using my name "Ryan" and the pronoun "he" six months ago. And now he had publicly acknowledged me as his son. It was amazing.

"Well, you certainly look like your dad," the older man said.

I looked up at my dad, and our eyes made contact. I smiled.

"I sure do."

When we sat down in front of my grandma's coffin, I began flipping through the program. Listed under my grandma's name were the survivors. I read down the list and saw my name listed correctly as my parents' son.

An image of our family tree popped into my head and I saw my old name being erased and my new name added there. I saw another branch being added for my partner and thought about branches for our kids, but my mind scribbled the extension of branches out. I knew my biology wasn't made for passing on genes, and I had lost the desire to be a traditional family unit with Michelle. I wasn't sure what that lost desire meant, but I couldn't bring myself to explore it at the time.

It was a long and hard struggle to get to this point in my life with my family. I could complain about the things that we went through, but I've learned that that's what families are there to do, experience change and hopefully not lose sight of what really matters—one another.

After the funeral I helped the other men carry my grandma's coffin to the hearse. I was very careful with how I picked up the heavy coffin and carried it. I tried to ignore the stares from people in the community who knew I had transitioned. I also tried to push out any thoughts I might harbor about what was running through their heads about my new physical appearance and suit.

When we reached the graveyard, I walked with my dad over to the hearse. Six of us waited to carry her coffin over to the grave, where she would be lowered to her final resting place. I ended up in the position where I would be one of the guys lifting the coffin onto the rollers and pulley system over the grave. I set my side down and began to push, but the coffin wouldn't budge. I started to feel perspiration drop from my forehead as I tried again. I felt like a failure, like a fraud. The funeral director apologized profusely as he messed with the rollers; apparently, they were broken. He started to push with my brother-in-law on the other side and I started to see the coffin lean toward me. I freaked out, envisioning my grandma literally rolling over in her grave. I grabbed the floral arrangement, which was sliding off the top, and the coffin itself to stabilize it.

Diverting a horrific scene, my brother-in-law then ran over to my side and picked up my end, moving it ahead of the broken roller. I watched as his broad shoulders, built from the overuse of supplements and hours in the gym, moved toward his neck as he lifted on what was supposed to be my end.

I could have done that, I thought.

Instead of fighting for my position, I fell back in line behind my brother-in-law and placed my hands on the rail. I gently pushed the coffin forward, but I felt like my hands weren't needed. I was just in the way.

I took a step back and looped around the other men and walked over by my dad. He looked down toward me and patted my shoulder.

My dad's gesture made me feel that Grandma's death reincarnated my birth into the family. This time I didn't come out as their daughter, but as their second son.

Good-bye, Grandma. It won't be the same without you, I thought as I held back tears. She never fully understood what was going on with me on the surface. I obeyed my parents' wish not to tell her about my transition and to pretend that nothing had changed.

Yet, after her death, everything began to change.

After reconciling my grandma's death, and having some time to process the interactions with my family, I was stuck asking, "What now?"

For the past five years, my identity had been wrapped up in my transition and the anticipation of all the physical changes that testosterone and surgeries would bring, as well as how my family would accept me. Now, besides the presence of more body and facial hair, I had nothing physical left to focus on. Also, with what appeared to be my family shifting toward broader acceptance, my emotional turmoil was lessening.

This lack of focus left me more aware of my life outside my transition and family, and it scared me. I now saw a guy stuck in a mundane life with an unromantic long-term relationship. I also recognized that besides work, my biggest recreational activity was still drinking. I needed a change and felt the only way to do that was to become more successful in my job.

Right after graduating from college, I was hired to do education and training predominantly with gay and lesbian issues. After I started on the job, I expanded the focus to include topics related to being bisexual, transgender, queer, or questioning. From spending time in the classrooms, I noticed that younger generations were expressing more diverse intersections of their identities that went beyond labels and boxes. I met youth who were questioning their orientation and/or gender, and so they were experimenting with different relationships or different clothing attire. I also met youth who, like me, identified as, "queer." At first I struggled with this term since it could be used in a derogatory manner, but I found that the youth saw it as empowering because it leaves a person's orientation undefined and open. The term fit with me because although my gender is fixed, my attraction to people is very fluid.

When I began working on transgender issues, I became ambitious and stated that I wanted the organization I worked for to serve the transgender community, which meant I wanted the medical services department to provide hormones for those transitioning, and I wanted to host a support group.

In order to do this, I began to network, research, and train my organizations' staff and those in the community who worked in human services. After meeting other organizations or professionals who were trans-friendly, I developed a resource list and became a point person in the transgender community. I saw myself as the hub, like Chicago O'Hare's airport. People came to me with questions, and I then referred them on to the provider or providers to help them. My provider list gained the attention and interests of several people, including a therapist who specialized in working with transgender clients. When she looked over my list, she recognized the desire to have more collaboration with other providers in the community.

Two years after the list had been created her desire moved into action the day she unknowingly pulled me out of a mindless daydream at work. It began when I heard a bell tone chime from my computer which caused me to notice a blue box that had popped up in the left-hand corner of the screen.

I had just received a new e-mail.

I clicked on the subject title *A Potential Task Force,* and began to read the content: *Hey, Ryan, For the past several months I've been wanting to reach out and see if you'd be interested in starting a task force with me for people who work with the transgender community. It seems like we all are doing such great things and I think it would be great if we could connect others to help the community! E-mail me back if you'd like to work with me on this. ~Lily.*

I was happily surprised by the e-mail. Over the years I'd referred several clients to her, but had never had personal contact. I e-mailed back: *Yes! Let's do it.*

I loved my job, but I was looking for a way to expand the breadth of work I did, and saw this as a way to begin that change.

Our first meeting was arranged in the basement of a bookstore I had never been to before. I wasn't very familiar with the bigger city; in fact, I avoided it because it overwhelmed me, so I arrived a half hour early for the meeting. Instead of just sitting around and waiting, I roamed through the bookstore and scanned the various titles in my two favorite sections, psychology and home improvements.

One of the reasons I wanted to buy an old house was because I loved to do home improvements. Working with a hammer and saw reminded me of the times when I worked beside my dad as a kid. As an adult, whenever I used my hammer, I always made sure to hold the handle near the end. My dad loved to share one of his childhood memories of his grandpa cutting off the handle of a hammer he was using because he was holding it too close to the top.

"If you aren't going to use it right, then there is no use to having the rest of the handle," his grandpa said.

Having bought a house built in 1900, there was never a time that I didn't have a home project in the works. Over the years, I had learned how to do a marginal job at drywalling and duct repair, so I loved to find books with new tips on how to improve my technique. I ended up buying a book that was geared toward old homes, with the hope that it would help me, but also because I felt nervous and needed something to read to calm my nerves. I was about to meet all of the professionals whom I would refer others to, but I didn't know any of them personally.

A few minutes before the meeting was supposed to begin, I went into the basement and waited. I saw that there was a restroom there, so I quickly ran in to use it before everyone else arrived. As the toilet was flushing, I reached over to the door handle, turned, and pushed, but it wouldn't budge. I pushed again without success, leading me into a panic. I didn't want to be known by all these people as "the guy who was stuck in the bathroom." I decided to put my shoulder into it and push as hard as I could. The door swung open after my third try and I stumbled out into the room. I looked around to see if anyone saw me, relieved to see I was still the only one down there. I sat down and composed myself at the table, acting like the restroom incident had never happened.

The first couple of people who showed up to the meeting were a professor, who had transitioned from male to female, and a therapist, who worked predominantly with the older transgender population. I handed my business cards to them and we chatted for a bit, before another woman came down the stairs.

She was wearing a pair of black slacks, which highlighted her long legs, a white blouse, and a black blazer. All of her limbs were long and lean, including her neck. She had the body of a ballerina, but I could tell by how she walked that she was a little clumsier than a gliding dancer. Her black hair was pulled back into a low-hanging ponytail, but I could make out a patch that was dyed pink in the back, which was on the opposite side from a patch of her bangs that was dyed purple. I immediately wanted to ask her why she dyed her hair with odd colors in odd places, but I didn't want to pry. Instead, I looked at the rest of her face. She had tortoiseshell glasses perched on her small nose and dark brown Gypsy eyes. When I looked at her, I kept seeing the actress Mary-Louise Parker, which made it hard for me to look away. I had had a crush on Mary-Louise since I was a teenager. It started with the movie *Fried Green Tomatoes,* and then continued with each new film or TV show I saw her in.

"Sorry I'm a little late, everyone! I'm Lily," she said.

I smiled when I heard her speak. She sounded like she was from Minnesota. Her *O*'s and *A*'s were both held out longer than the other vowels. She didn't look like most of the therapists I had known in the past, who either came off as the Mother Earth/hippy type or a nurturing mother ready to feed you warm cookies and give you a glass of ice-cold milk. Besides her clumsiness, she looked like she was more suited to be a lawyer. She was sleek, composed, and ambitious.

She sat down next to me and I caught a whiff of her perfume, which smelled more like mildly masculine soap. She looked over to me to shake my hand and thank me for agreeing to help her with the task force, and I felt my stomach cinch up. I was instantly nervous and intimidated by her. We both ran transgender support groups and I had this fear that she would judge my ability to facilitate a group—especially since she was the one with a degree in counseling; mine was in educational psychology.

After the meeting was over, everyone began scooting their chairs away from the table, except for me. I felt all of my joints lock up and my body sink farther onto the wooden chair. I watched as she pushed her chair in and hoped she would get caught up in conversation with one of the other departing members, ignoring me. Instead, she looked down at me. Our eyes made contact, and my face blushed.

"Should we set up a meeting to talk more about the organization of the group?" she asked as she slung a large black purse over her shoulder. Her arms scooped up the tablet and pen she had brought to take notes, and she pulled them up to her chest. I noticed her hands were also long and lean, matching the rest of her body.

"Yes, we should," I said matter-of-factly. I wanted to keep my cool and stay in business mode. I saw her as a business partner and someone I wanted to keep on my good side.

"How about we meet after our next meeting?"

It took me a second to process her question before grabbing my phone and scanning my calendar. It was one month away. I was looking forward to our meeting because I was curious about her occupational background. I knew that my work in the community was largely related to my own experiences, but I knew she wasn't trans-identified herself.

When we began meeting with each other, my intentions were to talk with her about the task force and get to know her background. These were my initial goals; but with each meeting we had, we ended up spending more time talking about random things not even related to transgender issues.

♂

By December, the winter's snow had successfully covered the ground and packed the streets. Traveling was becoming more difficult, but I still made it to the task force meetings each month. Lily and I planned to meet afterward to discuss a research project she was interested in conducting, and to talk about the newly launching hormone therapy services for transgender clients at my work.

I noticed that with each meeting that passed, my clothing choices shifted from button-up business shirts to tight T-shirts, even when the weather was negative degrees outside.

"So where do you want to go today?" she asked. She had on another business suit and high-heeled boots.

"You pick . . . and drive, if you wouldn't mind," I said.

A fresh round of snow had started to fall. By the time we reached her car, her windshield was covered. I sat down inside and looked around for her ice-scraper. She got into the driver's seat and started the ignition before reaching behind me.

I saw her pull out the ice-scraper, and I said, "I can scrape your windows for you, if you like."

"What?" she asked as she was stepping out of the car. "Oh, no. I can do it."

I felt like an ass as I watched her clear off the windshield. I was afraid she might have taken my offer out of context, as if I was suggesting that women couldn't clean off their own cars.

When she got back in the car, I started to stammer. "I didn't mean to suggest that you couldn't clean your own windshield. I—I was just trying to be nice, since you are driving."

She began to laugh. "You don't need to apologize. I'm a single woman. I'm just used to doing things on my own."

"Okay . . . I just want to make sure you don't think I belittle women or something."

"I don't think that at all." She shifted her car into gear and wove us through the icy streets.

I scouted a table as we entered the coffee shop, choosing one close to the restrooms because it was the only spot I felt had more privacy. I set my yellow notepad down on the surface and waited for her. She sat down across from me with a large sugar cookie and small coffee. I loved the fact that she loved cookies.

"So what's been going on with you this past month?" she asked as she dipped a piece of her cookie in her coffee.

"Not much," I said.

"I don't believe that. I don't even know when you find time to sleep with all of the work you do."

"Oh, I sleep!" I laughed. I felt a rush of warmth hit my body by her compliment. "What have you been up to?"

"Nothing too exciting," she said. "This past weekend I enjoyed spending time with two of my friends, whom I just adore. They've been together for over three years, and they're one of those couples where you know they just truly love each other."

I scoffed and said, "Yeah, wait until they hit six years."

"Whoa. Something going on in your life?" she inquired.

"I just feel like I could care less about my relationship. I hate this feeling and I keep saying it will go away, but it won't."

I began to question why I was sharing this information with her. Did I want her to know that I wasn't happy in the relationship, or did I just want someone to help me figure things out?

"You've been together six years. I'm guessing you're just going through an emotional divorce. Here look at this." She leaned over and grabbed my notepad and then started drawing three circles. She started to explain the ups and downs of emotional attachment in relationships, and I was trying to take in all of her views.

She finished explaining the circles and then said, "See, it's just an emotional divorce. . . . Give it time."

I looked at her and was taken aback by how caring she always came off.

"If you say so," I said while pulling the notepad closer to me and looking at the circles.

My silent mantra became *It's just an emotional divorce. It's just an emotional divorce.*

♂

I wanted to try and break the emotional divorce, so I decided that Michelle and I should buy a new bed. I realized that I was spending more time sleeping on our green couch in the family room, instead of in the bedroom. I decided that it was because the mattress was too old, and because we had spent our time and money decorating every room in the house except our master bedroom. I decided a new bed might bring a new spark to our relationship.

Sheer panic started to swirl around my body as I watched the deliverymen set up the bed. After they left, I went into our bedroom and looked at the cherry-colored sleigh bed. I became even more panicked when I realized that we had purchased all of the other furniture in the house together. The bed being loaded up into the delivery truck and taken away had been hers. When the deliverymen left, so did the last item that could be termed hers or mine, everything was now *ours*.

The only items needed to completely enmesh our worlds were a marriage certificate and wedding photos.

"This bed is so nice," Michelle said.

"Yeah . . . it is," I replied as I looked down at her left hand and noticed the ring I gave her the night she turned down my proposal.

In the past, I liked seeing the ring on her finger. It gave me hope that she would consider marriage in the future. That hope left my heart several months ago and I yearned to be brave enough to tell her about my struggles; but instead, I just smiled at her and left the room.

"Wow!" Michelle said as she touched the smooth woodwork.

I looked at her, the bed, and the room. I felt unsettled.

It's just an emotional divorce. It's just an emotional divorce.

I continued my mantra around Valentine's Day when I chose to go to a party by myself. I went partly because I wanted to see if people would hit on me. I also went because I knew Lily would be there, even though I figured she would be busy talking with the people she knew. I was surprised when she came up to me to say hi, and we ended up talking the rest of the night. As I left, I looked back at her and had the desire to hug her good-bye, but I resisted.

For Michelle's and my six-year anniversary, I decided to surprise her with a trip to Kansas City. I reserved a room in a fancy hotel and asked her to pack a bag.

"Where are we going?" she asked, excited by the thought of getting out of town.

"It's a surprise. Just pack your bag for the weekend, and have it ready to go after work."

We had gone to Kansas City for our first weekend getaway six years ago, so I thought being in the place where our relationship started to grow would rekindle my feelings for her.

After checking into the hotel, we lay down on the bed and I began to kiss her neck. Our intimacy had been reduced to hugs good-bye and an occasional "I love you." Her body quickly stiffened and her energy grew distant as I touched her, so I gave up. The rest of the trip I felt like I was just going through the motions with her.

On the drive home I had the desire to talk with her about our relationship. However, I feared if I started talking, all of the truths would come gushing out of me. I wasn't ready to accept the fact that we were done. We were supposed to be the couple that could beat all odds and make it through the transition.

♂

Since the trip to Kansas City didn't pan out the way I had hoped, I thought I would give us one more try by inviting her to join me in Philadelphia for a transgender health conference. She declined the invitation, leaving me to go on my own.

As I stood in the Chicago airport, waiting for my connecting flight, I heard a familiar voice say, "Hey."

I looked over my shoulder and saw Lily standing next to me.

I had suggested the conference to the task force in previous meetings, and so she had decided to check it out.

"H-hey!" I stuttered back, nervous to see her.

"Looks like we are on the same flight," she said.

"It does," I replied.

I was distracted by the announcer's voice calling off seating zones. I'm the type of person who likes to get on the airplane as quickly as possible, so I have a better chance of shoving my carry-on in the bin above my seat.

"I'm sorry . . . I need to get on right now."

"Oh, okay," she said as an old guy next to her started to ask her a question.

I felt horrible for abandoning her in the terminal, so I watched for her to board. A few minutes later she started to walk past me. I waved at her and blurted out, "I'll wait for you after I get off the plane."

"Okay," she said as she moved past me. I noted that she was located four seats back.

I kept my word and waited in the Philadelphia terminal for her. Through the line of people, I could see her black hair bobbing up and down. Her long legs moved her past the two older people shuffling slowly in front of her. I nodded my head at her and smiled. She smiled back and began walking toward me, hands clasping a book and shoulders weighed down by two purse-like bags.

It was nice to see her in jeans and a T-shirt instead of her professional clothes. I felt less intimidated by her.

"See, I told you I would wait," I said as she approached me.

"Sure, Sallans. I know you just want to ditch me," she joked. This was the first time I had heard her use my last name.

"I wouldn't ditch you." I reached back and grabbed the handle of my roller bag. "Uh, would you like to ride the train into town with me?" I asked.

"Yeah, I just need to grab my bag from baggage claim."

We wove through the crowds toward baggage claim. I stood back and watched her search for her bag on the rotating track. A large red suitcase, packed to the point that the sides pushed out, came up on the belt. She reached out. As she pulled it off the conveyer belt, the luggage appeared to be heavier than she was.

"Do you want me to help you with your bag?" I asked as she rolled it toward me.

"No, I got it," she said.

Anxious about missing the next train, I spun around and led us back to where we could hitch a ride into town. We took our place next to each other on a bench, which allowed us to look out the window and watch the scenery as we made our way into the heart of the city.

"Where is the hotel you are staying at?" I asked.

"Uh, I don't know exactly."

"What? You don't know where it is located?" I felt my anxiety rising for her. I always mapped things out before I left on a trip.

"Nah, I figured I'd just wander the streets until I find it. That's what I always do. It's no big deal."

"Ah, man. You're killing me," I said.

"Well, it's a good thing we aren't together. The way I travel would drive you nuts," she said as she leaned her shoulder in to tap mine.

I felt a rush of sadness when I looked back toward her.

"I'd just plan it for us," I quickly assured her.

Neither of us had ever outwardly expressed interests in each other, but her comment seemed to have ended it before we could even start.

The announcer's voice called out the station we would be stopping at. I let her and her overstuffed suitcase step off the train ahead of me. I shook my head because in a way she was right. She would drive me nuts if we traveled together. I never checked bags because it slowed down the time we could get to places.

We stood in the middle of the train station with people in business suits rushing past us on all sides. I pulled out my cell phone and tried to pull up my Internet so that I could look up the address to her hotel. My phone wasn't responding, and the announcer called out the train that I was supposed to board was approaching the station. I looked at her and stuttered out, "I—I . . . my phone isn't working, and my train is coming." I felt my heartbeat increase and I started to shake my phone—a pointless gesture since shaking it wouldn't make the Internet go any faster.

My ears started to turn red and sweat beaded on my forehead as I looked at the frozen screen. I wanted to direct her to her hotel. I wanted to help her—even though I could tell I was the one who was distressed; she seemed pretty calm.

"Just go," she said as she waved her hand outward. "I'll find it. If I can't, I'll just ask."

"Okay," I said before turning and running down the stairs to my boarding spot.

After I got out of the station and through the tunnels, I pulled up her hotel's address. I felt like I should have walked with her and made sure she got to the hotel safely. After finding the address, I texted her, *Did you get there okay?* Then I sent her the address.

While talking with my friends and drinking a beer, I kept checking my phone by my side. Finally, after an hour, she sent back a message: *Yes! I got a little lost but found it. Are we still on for tomorrow?*

Before leaving for the trip, we had e-mailed back and forth making plans for a tour of a penitentiary that was said to be haunted. I was thrilled when she said she loved paranormal activity as much as I did.

Yep. I'll find you at the conference and we can go from there, I texted back.

♂

I waited for her outside of the conference center after the first session. I was nervous to hang out with her, and do things that I would normally do with Michelle. My nerves melted as I saw Lily emerge from the building and walk up toward me. I smiled as I looked at her hands clasped around two small shoulder straps that led back to an orange bag she was wearing like a backpack. It looked more like a bag one would take to the beach, instead of one used as an everyday purse. I liked her little quirks. Other women I knew always wanted purses that matched their outfits. Lily just wanted something that was convenient to carry and could hold what she needed.

"You ready to go?" I asked as she walked over to me.

"Yep. Do you know how to get there?" she asked.

"Uh, I know it's in that direction," I said as I pointed toward the east. "So let's just start walking, and I'll try to pull up the navigation on my phone."

"Okay . . . or we could just ask someone," she said.

"Nah, my phone will work."

After twenty minutes of walking in circles and along a busy highway, I gave up using my phone, and surrendered to the fact that asking someone would be easier. When I showed Lily that I was ready to surrender, she walked over to two women and asked them where we should go. They pointed south, and said to go seven blocks. Ten minutes later we arrived in front of the prison. Lily looked over to me and said, "See how easy that was. It's called the old-fashioned GPS."

I looked up at her and tried to hide how turned on I was by her sassiness. "Yeah, yeah," I playfully threw back at her.

We walked under the arch of the prison entrance and past the rusted gates into an updated room filled with souvenirs. We paid the admission fee and were given headsets and a recorder, which played commentary as we walked in the prison yard and through the long hallways stacked one to three stories tall, with steel doors every six feet. While in the yard, or inside one of the cells, we would talk about the experiences men and women must have felt while confined within the shallow cavities.

As we moved along, I laughed when I noticed that she liked to touch things to get a sense of their texture. She kept running her long fingers over the broken pieces of stone, across the steel and wooden doors, and on top of the tree roots that were pushing through the walls. I could feel her slightly closer to me when we entered death row, or the dark basements that were used for solitary confinement. When she inched closer, I had to remind myself that I couldn't reach out toward her and pull her against my body.

We left the prison and went to an Irish pub for a late lunch. We sat with our wine and beer and talked about ghosts. She began telling me stories about the house where she grew up and how she remembered a male ghost walking down the hallways and lingering in the kitchen when her mom would make dinner. I was fascinated by her stories and realized I didn't want our day to end. I found myself feeling like I was a character in one of my books, interacting with the person I desired.

By the time our three days together had passed, and I was boarding the train to go back to the airport, I felt something fluttering inside. These were sexual feelings—feelings that hadn't pulsed through my veins in a very long time.

I immediately felt guilty and insecure.

I couldn't have a crush on one of my colleagues.

Especially when I was in a relationship, right?

The emotional high I had experienced in Philadelphia, while spending time with Lily, slowly wore off back home. As the good feelings left, I started to experience an increase in guilt. Instead of addressing my emotions, I buried my head in the sand and continued to text Lily from time to time to stay connected. After a month of random texts, our conversations became more constant.

The guilt I was experiencing had begun to weaken. It nearly came to a stop the day I visited Michelle at her office and realized we both needed a change in our lives. My epiphany occurred when she asked me to sit in her office chair to see what her perspective was when working with clients. I looked around and noticed all of the pictures she had posted on a corkboard above her computer. I smiled when I saw our dogs and her niece and nephews, but I became expressionless when I landed on a photo of me before my transition, holding the dog we had to put down several years prior, due to her aggression.

"Why do you have that photo up?" I asked while pointing. All I could feel was disgust when I saw it.

"I like it," she said.

"That photo is from the past. Why can't you have a new one up?"

"Because it's one of the last memories I have left," she said. Her smile turned downward and the tone in her voice expressed how sad she was not to have me as a woman.

I realized all of the work we did in the relationship surrounding the transition would never take away the pain she had from not being with a woman. I knew that I would never fully be seen as *me* in her eyes, which could be one of the reasons I didn't feel like I knew myself anymore.

"Whatever," I said. "I need to go back to work."

I got up to leave, but was stopped by her asking for a hug. I leaned down and patted her back. It was the type of hug I gave people I didn't know.

My "emotional divorce" from her became final at that moment. I began to carry my cell phone around the house so that I didn't miss a text, if one was sent, from Lily. Our conversations became more suggestive and flirtatious with each day that passed, but never overly direct to what we were feeling.

With summer almost over, I couldn't handle it anymore. I wanted to be out in the sun with her and missed being around her. So on a Saturday morning, I sent a text, *Wanna go to the lake?*

She texted back immediately: *Wish I could but I have to work.*

I do too. Let's just play hooky and go.

Oh, that sounds like much more fun! Tempting, but no.

Okay, I texted before giving up for the day.

That evening I was sitting in my recliner watching Shark Week on TV. Michelle was putting together an outfit for a costume-themed party that one of our friends was throwing for his birthday. The theme for the party was to come as a fantastic failure. I had decided earlier that night I wasn't in the mood to go, even though I had my character picked out: George Michael.

As I was watching a shark thrust through the chum-filled waters, I started to receive text messages from Lily.

The ending of one of them said, *God, I want to get out of town.*

From the knots in my stomach and the increased suggestions I was sending through text, I knew it was time to quit beating around the bush with her. I needed to take a risk, so I texted back, *Come down here!*

Farther than Lincoln, she replied.

I understand that. Philly was the last place I have been.

The message hung in cyberspace. A few minutes passed before I got the reply: *Where are we going tonight?*

Would you really come down?

I waited a few minutes again before my phone vibrated.

Sure, she responded.

I jumped out of my seat. I couldn't believe she was driving down late at night to see me. I ran upstairs and started to change my outfit.

Michelle was on the bed, deciding what shoes would go with the costume I had helped her design earlier that night. She had on blue jeans and a white tank top that had handwritten scribbles across the front,

President of the Abstinence Club. Stuffed under her tank top were a pillow, wrapped in duct tape, and two pieces of panty hose filled with rice for breasts.

"I know I'm not going to the party. . . . I don't feel like being around a bunch of people, but Lily is coming down and we are just going to have a drink at the Starlite."

"Just the two of you?" she asked. She looked at me and inspected my face. Her squinted eyes and turned-down lips made me wonder if she knew why I wanted to go.

"Yes . . . do you want to go?" I asked, knowing that she hated going to the Starlite. It was a dark martini lounge, underneath a restaurant in the city, and not very entertaining for people who didn't drink.

"No. . . ," she said as she watched me tossing through my T-shirts, trying to find an outfit I felt comfortable in. "Do you have a crush on her?"

"What? No," I said. I could say "no" without lying because I knew I didn't have a crush on her. It was more.

"I don't like her. I'm not intimidated by many people, but I am by her," Michelle said.

I hated to hear that. I knew I was feeling the same thing she had felt for Ellen four years ago. It wasn't fair, and I started to feel like I had kept her from something I wouldn't allow myself to be kept from.

"It will be okay," I said.

As I watched Michelle pull away in her car, I had a feeling she left for the party that night knowing what was coming.

After she left, I jumped in my car and drove downtown. I anxiously waited for Lily at a dark street corner, so that I could escort her down the stairs and into the martini lounge. After a few minutes I could make out her walk and a white blouse in the faint distance. My heart gained a few extra beats as I saw her getting closer.

"Ryan . . . what are you doing?"

My heart stopped. I began to question if I really heard a voice or if I was just imagining one. I slowly turned and looked down over my shoulder and saw LeeAnn standing beside me. Over her shoulder I could see her husband inside a restaurant, talking with the hostess. I couldn't believe that out of all the times to run into someone I knew, it had to be right at that moment. I glanced around to see if anyone else I knew was around. I began to wonder whether this chance meeting was a sign. And if it was a sign, was it telling me not to be in hiding anymore?

"I'm meeting someone down here for a drink," I said, hoping she wouldn't pry more.

Her eyes looked like a kitten getting ready to pounce on a toy. With a smile she asked, "Who?"

"Lily," I said.

She knew who I was talking about. Apparently, I talked about Lily a lot.

At that moment her husband came out to join us. He reached his hand out to shake mine and asked, "What are you doing out this late?"

"He's meeting with Lily," LeeAnn said. Now I had two pairs of playful kitten eyes looking at me.

"Hey," Lily said as she walked up next to me.

"Hey," I said, trying to act cool. I introduced everyone before saying, "We need to go. . . . See you at work on Monday."

As we walked away, I could feel their curiosity piercing my back, and I could only imagine what their conversation was going to be during their dinner.

I picked out a table in the lounge that would distance us from the larger crowds. The wall sconce above the table lit up her face and white peasant blouse. Our conversation started much like our texting had, very casually.

After having a few sips of my martini, I blurted out, "Do you realize we've texted for over twelve hours over the past three days?"

"Really?" she said with a deadpan look.

"Yes, really."

"What do you think it means?" she asked as she straightened her back and crossed her arms on her chest. I could tell she was nervous. I even picked up on a little guilt. Our friendship began after I opened up about my relationship and my struggles; now I sensed that she feared being seen as the homewrecker.

"What do you think it means?" I played the old therapist trick and threw it back at her. (I knew what it meant, but wanted to make sure she felt the same way.)

"I think it means there is something between us. . . ." Her voice trailed off.

"I do, too."

We both sat there, in silence. It felt like we had both received unsettling news and our bodies were still in shock, unable to process the next steps.

"You know we can't do anything about these feelings when you are in a relationship." Her voice broke the silence.

"I know. I wouldn't want to, anyway. I want us to do this right," I said.

"I'm going to let you figure out what that means for you."

"I will."

A woman wearing a black button-up shirt and bright blue necktie interrupted the awkwardness. "Can I get you both one more round?"

I nodded my head yes; while Lily shook hers no.

"I still can't believe this." She threw her hands up toward her face and pushed them under her glasses. Her glasses went up and rested on her forehead as she leaned back in her chair. "Oh, my God," she breathed out with a sigh as she straightened her posture. She dropped her hands back down and her glasses fell back into place. "You know I'm going to be seen as the black widow that's crawled my way in."

"We both know that isn't true," I said before taking a swig of the mostly olive-juice martini.

"It doesn't matter what is true. It's what people want to see."

"I'm sorry. We didn't go into this with intentions. . . . We just . . . fit."

I lifted my martini glass up and took another swig. I looked around the bar and noticed the crowd was starting to pick up even more. Being a regular there, I didn't want to run into any more people I knew, so I leaned in toward Lily and said, "I think we should go."

"Yeah," she agreed.

I let the last drops of my martini run down my throat before pulling out my credit card and holding it up for the server. I felt my pocket vibrate while waiting for the receipt. I pulled out my phone and looked down at the glowing screen. I had received a text message from LeeAnn that read: *You know curiosity is pulling us to going down to the Starlite for a drink, but we'll refrain.* I quickly clicked off the screen and stuck it back into my pocket.

"You ready?" I asked as I picked up my wallet and shoved it into my pocket with my phone.

We left the basement and entered the breezy night. We began wandering the block; no real destination in mind. I just knew that I didn't want to leave her side. I wanted to reach out my hand and grab hold of hers, but I didn't feel right touching her yet.

After circling around the block, we ended up stopping at a fountain. Water ran from a large barrel, tipped on its side and into a small wading pool. The rippling water was the only sound and movement around us. Both of our bodies were tense.

"May I walk you back to your car?"

I looked at her and tried to imagine what it would be like to be out with her and seen as her boyfriend. With her heels on, she was a couple of inches taller than I was, making me feel like less of a man.

"Sure," she said.

I noticed that her body language was closed off and her face was pale. Her body was shaking, and so was mine. The shaking lessened as we made our way farther away from the shopping district, and onto the side roads lined with factories closed for the night.

The darkness wrapped around us like a security blanket. I felt more anonymous the farther we walked, sheltered from other people's judgments. The protection of the night increased my desire to pull her close, but I continued to resist.

As we got to her car, we stood there for a moment. She leaned against the driver's-side door and let out a nervous chuckle.

"So what's next?"

"I need to break up with Michelle. . . ."

My face became pale as I heard those words come out of my mouth. I looked up at her, but she had shifted her focus toward the ground. I knew she felt as sick as I did. I wanted to kiss her, but instead reached up and gave her an awkward hug, which lasted less than a second, before stepping away.

This was the second time I had hugged her; the first time was after a night out in Philadelphia.

"Text me when you get home."

"Okay," she said as she opened her car door and sat down behind the steering wheel. It was still all too surreal to understand fully.

I made it home before Michelle. I felt relieved, knowing I was the first one there. It gave me time to go to bed and not have to deal with my new reality. My stomach tightened when I remembered we'd be going together the next day to celebrate Jake's birthday at the zoo.

I had noticed that the more distance I tried to put between Michelle and me, the more she would try to bring us closer by holding me, hugging me, or saying that she loved me. I knew I couldn't be close to her at the zoo. Any touch she gave me would make me feel like I was cheating on Lily, so I confided in a friend about what was happening before we all left that day.

I chose a mutual friend of ours, knowing he could be there to support Michelle and also respect me for the choices I was making. Having lived with us for six months that past year, he knew and saw the breakdown of the relationship. It was good to hear his perspective because it confirmed what I was afraid to accept, up until the night before.

While walking through the different animal attractions at the zoo, I resisted texting Lily. I was able to hold out until that evening when I wrote, *My stomach is full of butterflies; my heart is aching because I'm here and there. I can't stop thinking about you right now.*

My butterflies became even more jumbled when I read her response: *I've done a lot of thinking between my sleepless night and today. I have some things that need to be said, so I think talking tomorrow is important.*

I felt like someone had punched me in the stomach, and I began to wonder if she was having second thoughts about us. I wanted to respect her request, but my fears pushed me to reach out: *One more text, then I'll leave you alone. . . . Have you changed your mind about us?*

I couldn't stand the thought of losing her before I even had her.

No. And I'm not trying to be cryptic, but there is only so much one can communicate via text.

I didn't sleep that night and couldn't concentrate at work the next day. I found myself lying on the floor by my friend Lisa's desk. She had known there was something going on between Michelle and me for the past year. LeeAnn, who caught me out with Lily on Saturday night, kept running over to Lisa's office to check on me.

After going back and forth as to whether I should call Lily, I summoned the courage to press her name on my phone's screen.

"Hello?" her voice sounded weak.

"Hey," I said. "I hate this." I reached over and turned off the lights in my office before lying on the floor.

"I do, too. I can't focus. I can't eat. I feel like puking."

"I'm sorry. What did you want to say to me today that you couldn't by text?" I asked, scared of what had grown in her mind.

"I just want to make sure we are both honoring the process, and that you take the time you need," she said. "I don't want to be a rebound person for you, and I also want us to respect the ending of your long-term relationship."

"I get it," I said.

I hated that I was in a relationship, and feared it would overshadow the love story developing between us. "I just want you to know that the breakup would happen with or without you in the picture."

"Yeah, from what you told me, it should. I just worry that you'll rush into something with me, and then end up hurting me. I'm taking a risk on you."

"I hate to think of me as a risk. I won't hurt you."

I turned onto my other side and imagined her lying there next to me.

"You never know. . . ," she countered.

"Well, I guess risks are just part of being in a relationship."

"Yeah, you're right."

"I know I am. I'll talk with you soon, okay?"

"Okay," she said before hanging up.

I stayed on the floor in my office until Lisa grabbed me and pulled me out to a restaurant for dinner. I then went over to her house for a beer before summoning the energy to drive my Jeep back home.

I knew Michelle would be sitting on the couch, waiting for me. She had been sensing something was going on for several months.

In the past when she asked, "Are we okay?"

I'd respond, "Yep."

My brother was going through a divorce, so I used the ending of his twenty-year marriage as an excuse for my distance. I was now at the point that I couldn't keep it up any longer. When I walked up onto the porch, I looked down at my feet and noticed the peeling paint on the old-wood boards.

I should have sanded and repainted the porch before today, I thought as I pushed open the oak door and moved through our threshold. I spent the summer completing some of the bigger projects on our home in order to improve the curb appeal. I had hoped that fixing things in and around the home would make me feel better about my relationship. But now, I knew that I was fixing tangible things, because they were easier than trying to fix a relationship that was beyond repair. Our dogs, a black greyhound and a compact Lab, whooshed against my legs.

"Hey," I heard Michelle's voice say. It sounded weak and insecure.

She was sitting around the corner, rocking back and forth in my beat-up recliner. *The X-Files* was softly playing on the TV.

"Hey," I said back, also insecure and weak. I pushed the dogs aside and walked over to the couch. I sat next to the pillow I used to rest my head on at night. I pulled a blanket over my lap.

As she got up and sat down next to me on the couch, I couldn't even make eye contact with her.

"What's going on?" she asked.

I turned my head away from her and stared at the gray walls, the walls we had painted together.

"Come on, tell me," she prodded.

Tears started to drip slowly down my cheeks. Besides my grandma's funeral and our first breakup, I hadn't been able to cry in years.

She noticed me wipe away the few drops and then grabbed a pillow to wrap her arms around. Her lip began to quiver and her nose started to twitch when she asked, "Do you want to break up?"

Hearing her ask me what I didn't have the strength to say caused me to lose it. The small tears turned into a gush as I shook and repeatedly said, "I'm sorry. I'm sorry. I'm sorry."

"No, no, no," she said. "I don't want to break up. We were doing good. I was ready to marry you."

She turned onto her side, breathing heavily and crying.

"We have to," I said through my tears. "I love you, but we aren't meant to be together."

I apologized some more and watched her rock back and forth before she jumped off the couch. She grabbed her phone and headed out to the front porch. I remained in the same spot for fifteen minutes before going out with a box of tissues and a glass of water for her.

I slowly sat down next to her, cautious of her feelings and her potential desire for me just to stay away. We rocked back and forth on the swing in silence for a few minutes before she asked, "What changed between us?"

I didn't have a concrete answer for her.

"A lot of things have changed. Our relationship isn't a romantic one. It hasn't really ever been. We are great at being friends and roommates, and we have a lot of fun and know how to laugh, but we aren't romantic. . . . I can't be in a relationship that lacks passion."

I knew that if we had passion, we would have had a long life together; but a close friendship wasn't enough for me any longer.

"I'm okay with the way things are," she said.

"I'm not, and I think you aren't really—deep down inside."

The sad memories started to flash through my brain like an animated picture book: our struggles to find sexual compatibility, our increased distance with each year that passed, our annoyances with little habits exploding into arguments, my inability to vocalize an "I love you" when I heard her say it in a questioning tone, and lastly my increased desire to be with another woman—something I couldn't tell her at that moment.

"What's next?" she asked.

I hadn't thought too far ahead, but I knew I wanted her to have the house and the pets. I didn't feel I was in a place to be able to give the pets what they needed, and I felt like I couldn't stay in Lincoln any longer.

I had spent fourteen years in the city, most of which revolved around depression and suicide ideation or attempts.

"We'll figure all of the details out in a couple of days. Let's just try to get some sleep tonight."

She grabbed her water and went upstairs. I grabbed the pillow she had brought out and retreated to the couch.

I picked up my phone and typed, *I've told her. . . . I'll talk to you tomorrow a.m.* I then sent it to Lily. It was close to midnight, so I didn't expect a reply. But just like me, she hadn't been sleeping for weeks.

Okay, thinking of you. Talk to you tomorrow was all she texted back.

It ended up being the last full night I spent in the house.

The next morning I placed my hand on the silver doorknob, pulled it open, and stepped away from a place I had called home—a place I had been fixing up for over five years, and a place that had sheltered friends we had grown to call family.

I became scared when I realized that falling in love with someone who lived in a city an hour away from my home would not only take me away from my familiar surroundings, but it would also take me away from everyone I loved. It would mean separating the family we had built. I could only hope that when everyone received the news, they would forgive me and recognize how much I had struggled with accepting the truth.

Needing some time to process all of the rapid changes, I waited two more days before driving up to see Lily. My heart was torn in two. One part felt destroyed and broken by the reality of losing someone so integral to my life. The other part felt elated, nervous, and curious about what the future would bring.

"I can't believe you're here" were the first words out of Lily's mouth as she swung open the door to her house and pulled me inside.

She wasn't wearing her glasses, allowing me to peer more deeply into her eyes. I couldn't get over how dark they were, and felt as if I could fall into them and never find my way out.

Softly strung acoustics and male voices streamed from her CD player and enveloped our bodies as time continued to pass. The music held us in place in the doorway. We kissed for the first time and clung to each other, as if we were preparing for an unknown force to swoop in and try to tear us apart.

I felt strange kissing her. Michelle hated to kiss, besides small pecks on the lips. I never knew if this was just her preference, or if she thought I was a horrible kisser.

While kissing Lily, I knew I had met my match. Just like everything else that had evolved between us, kissing her was intuitive.

As we held each other, I heard "I love you" unconsciously slip from my lips.

I wanted to reach out and pull it back in, scared of rushing into another relationship, but it felt right. Throughout my life I restricted my thoughts and emotions until I would hit points of self-destruction: my eating disorder, the Swiss Army knife that I ran over my arms with quick and jagged cuts, my overdose on pills filled with ephedrine, and my bouts of depression that isolated me from the outer world. Like a cat with nine lives, I was teetering on number nine. This was my last chance to move past my fears and toward self-actualization.

Whether Lily represented the world where fear ruled and claimed me in self-defeat, or she was part of my path where fear was a stepping-stone toward self-actualization, was something I still needed to discover.

On the surface she appeared to ignore my unconscious slip while she leaned her head back to get a fuller glimpse of me.

"I just want to sit down and breathe you in." She slipped her fingers into the palm of my hand and began pulling me toward the couch. "I can't believe you're really here."

"I can't believe it, either," I said as we continued to kiss.

A love story was created that night; and with each night that passed, we were able to experience more raw and passionate emotions.

When I looked at her, I saw "all woman"; and the way she held me made me feel all man. With her, I forgot about my scars, my bi-monthly injections of testosterone, and my surgeries. This was ironic, since my transgender identity and the work I do relating to it was the reason we met.

Lily saw me as Ryan, just Ryan.

Wrapped up in the whirlwind of love, I pulled further away from my friends. A new identity was beginning to form within me, and I needed the space to explore it. I wasn't able to do that when I was around memories of my past, and close to places where I could play out my old patterns and behaviors.

I was starting a new transition in my life by moving into a relationship with someone who's always known me as Ryan, and being in a city that didn't know me at all. During this particular transition, however, I was shedding an identity of self-defeat, instead of the body parts that hid my true gender.

Over the course of the next few months, my boxes filled with books and tools—the only possessions I took from my house—had found their way into Lily's basement. I needed a place to store everything, and her unfinished basement had plenty of room.

I spent most nights with her and got up before the sun rose each morning to make the dreaded drive back to Lincoln, where I worked. I hated the drive and the miles I was putting on my car, so I asked my supervisor if I could be transferred to the new office. They happily agreed to move me, since they needed more educators in Omaha, where Lily lived.

I loved many aspects of my job; but after I stepped foot into my new office, I realized that I loved my coworkers, Lisa and LeeAnn, even more and I missed them. My body felt cold, which numbed my mind as I made my way to a cubicle with a blank spot for my nameplate.

I looked around and saw the top of a few heads swaying back and forth between their phones and computer screens, dozens of other cubicles sat empty—much like the energy in the room. I sat down in front of my new computer and looked at the screen. The fluorescent lights buzzing above my head and sounds of the other staff chatting on their phones distracted me from being able to concentrate.

Without my office with four walls and a door, and the cheery voices of my friends, I felt lost and displaced. This new office represented everything I hated about the workforce today: tiny cubicles decorated with tacky photos and obnoxious toys, no real interactions between the staff, just sad faces under yellow lights getting their time in before they could go home.

I knew I didn't fit with the organization anymore and I needed a change.

I texted Lily, *I hate this.*

After my first day, instead of going into the office, I spent most days at Lily's to complete my work. Each time I had to sit in the office, I felt like crawling out of my skin. After two months of struggling with the adjustment, I knew I needed to move out from underneath the security blanket that my job gave me and step out into the world of self-employment.

♂

I had been building my private business after appearing in *Gender Rebel*. It began when an out-of-state college had asked me to speak; then the next year two colleges contacted me, and then three. The trend has continued to build with each passing year. I loved the travel, the students, and doing what I do best: storytelling and educating.

My love for this life was one I felt awkward talking about with Michelle. After she had appeared with me in the documentary, she began to pull away from being interested in my work. It wasn't because she didn't support me, but rather because she didn't want to be a part of my public identity and had no desire to be the poster child for partners of transgender individuals.

I knew that Lily would want to have some privacy, but I also knew she would be present and open when needed during my public appearances. We had already conducted several trainings in various states on transgender issues. Our work had brought us together.

I found myself pulling even further away from my friends as I prepared to turn in my resignation letter. They began questioning my sanity and my reasoning, since they saw my life as completely changing. A few people started calling me "asshole"; the others were concerned that I was manic. I allowed their fears and opinions to touch me, but I didn't allow them to penetrate my skin. I saw the process as growing pains.

My friendships slowly started to redefine themselves, and some ended with me being seen as the estranged family member. I was estranged not only with people I had called friends, but also with the people in the local transgender community.

When I left my position at work, where I dedicated my time to LGBTQ advocacy, I also left my role as a support group facilitator and as a representative within community groups. Leaving behind everything I worked so hard to create caused me to struggle with feelings of vulnerability and irrelevance, especially when I heard of new people stepping into my old roles. I felt like I was no longer needed. I had left my community and moved into one where I felt like an intruder.

Lily quickly picked up on my sadness and began to worry about what would become of us. I felt her pulling away, afraid of being hurt. That pained me even more. I knew sitting around and feeling sorry for myself or scared of never finding future work was not the right approach, so I began hitting the online pavement.

I created blogs, started filming YouTube videos, hired a manager, and created a consulting business. Through my online outreach I continued to work with both local and international transgender individuals and their friends. Over the years I've mentored hundreds of people worldwide. My energy gets replenished when I run into people at conferences who mention I had helped them years ago.

"How do you do it, Ryan?" Lisa once asked me.

I looked over at her and saw a softer-featured Kathy Griffin.

Her hair was a shade of pomegranate and swirled down slightly past her shoulders. Her bangs were cut evenly across. She was sitting on the couch in Lily's and my living room.

When I moved away, Lisa and I started scheduling sleepovers so we could continue to stay in touch.

"How do I do what?" I asked back.

"How do you just allow some leap of faith? You always seem to go off and do some of the most crazy and random stuff, and always seem to succeed at it?"

"I don't know." I shrugged my shoulders and raised my hands to either side. "From all of these years, I've just learned to follow my gut."

"Well, that is one good gut you have then," she said as she shook her head. Her eyes widened as she thought about all of the changes she saw me go through over the years. She looked overwhelmed.

My skin prickled with goose bumps.

Most leaps I have taken have scared me shitless, but I refused to let fear hold me back, including fears surrounding love. Lily's Italian blood and need to explore every emotion, coupled with my Irish blood's propensity to just drink beer and avoid anything awkward, led us to a lot of challenges. Through our arguments I discovered that I'm good at taking on big life changes, but I'm weak when it comes to the small challenges in life—especially those that affect other people.

I've often felt like a protector in Lily's and my relationship, but her emotional reactions to my avoidance of certain situations, where I felt uncomfortable or insecure, has made me feel like a coward.

The opportunity for me to regain my dignity with my friends, and prove myself to Lily, presented itself close to a year after my breakup with Michelle.

♂

While scrolling through my Facebook page, I noticed that I was invited to a good-bye party for the same friend who had thrown the party the night Lily and I expressed our feelings toward each other. I avoided pressing the attending button, afraid to face the community I had left. That evening, while sitting on the patio, I made the mistake of mentioning the party to Lily.

"So there is a going-away party tomorrow night for my friend Ryan in Lincoln," I said.

"Really, when?" she asked.

"I didn't look, because I'm not going."

"What?" she asked in disbelief. "Oh, my God, Ryan. He's one of your friends, and you may not see him again. Why wouldn't you go?" Her face tensed up and her head slightly twitched. She was upset with me.

"I'm sure I'll see him again," I said. I looked down at the bricks below our feet, scared to make eye contact with her disbelief. "Plus I don't know who will be there."

I searched for a reason not to go, and then blurted out, "What if Michelle is there or some of our friends that I haven't seen since I left? I don't want to make people feel awkward."

"Oh, get over it, Sallans," she said, disappointed in my weakness.

"I just don't want to go," I lamely replied.

"All right, fine. Your friends deserve better than that, though. . . ." Her voice trailed off.

I hated when she did that, but I hated even more that she was right.

The bugs were starting to bite at our legs, so we headed back inside for the night. While she went upstairs to the bathroom, I pulled my laptop onto my lap and reached out to click on the attending button.

Later in the evening I received a text from Michelle: *Hey, I see you are going to be at the party tomorrow. Are you staying over? I thought we could go to the bank Saturday to finish the paperwork for the house.*

Eager to get the process done, and to have my name off the house loan, I texted back, *I am going. We can talk about it at the party if you want.*

K was all I received in response.

When Michelle arrived at the party, I noticed her hair was longer and dyed a lighter shade of blond. She wore a golfer cap tilted to the side. Her cheeks had a glow to them—one I saw here and there when we were together. I waited for her to make her way over to me; we ended up talking the rest of the night.

"You're happy, right?" I asked.

"Yeah, I am. Are you?" Her voice was softer, and her glow

changed. The stress of keeping up a house and caring for the animals on her own showed on her face.

"I am," I replied.

In the past I would have been scared to talk about my feelings. I was carrying guilt and the fear that Michelle saw me as the husband and father who abandoned his whole family when times got too hard.

"You know I still think about you. I just want the best for you . . . and me," I said.

It was strange to lose daily contact with someone who was so prominent in my life. We met when we were in our early twenties and helped each other grow into adults. I knew that even though we had ended our relationship, it was one I am happy I had in my life.

"I know. Me too," she said.

Before signing the papers the next morning, we went out to breakfast with our friends and old roommates who had lived in the home she was taking over, Jake and Tyler. I sat back for a moment and watched everyone talk around the table; hand gestures played out stories that were being shared.

Laughter bounced off our bodies as we talked about memories from the past and recent adventures that we had traveled alone. It felt good to be around my old friends. With all of the changes I had gone through, it was nice to be around people who were familiar to me. While my friend Tyler retold a story of drama between the gays of Lincoln the night before, I found myself butting in and making wisecrack jokes about his own sex life or, as I sometimes joked, lack thereof.

Tyler looked at me and said, "Ryan, you're an ass . . . and that's why we love you." We always had an endearing way of cracking jokes at each other that others would think were offensive, but to us it was a way to say, "I love you, man."

Tyler's response caused Jake to bust in with his Krusty the Clown laugh from *The Simpsons,* which then shifted our story to his recent camping adventures. Michelle and I looked at each other and smiled. The warmth from Tyler's and Jake's laughter covered my fear that they had lost interest in us.

A new fear encroached when I wondered if my life with Lily could ever be a part of us. I looked away from everyone and caught my reflection held within the tin of the old lamp that sat on the table. I saw everyone else's features also reflected in the curvature of the glass and smiled.

I felt peaceful and assured that like me, my chosen family was going to be all right. As time moves on, I know we'll all have our own individual leaps to make—some of us will make it easily to the other side, while others will waver and scramble to get our footing—but in the end, all I can hope for is that our transitions in life and love will lead us to a point where we feel whole and complete.

I used to believe that the only way I could feel comfortable and accepting of myself was to have both of my parents express full acceptance of their second son. I have been preparing for this ever since I first donned a cape and ran around my childhood bedroom. Over the years, I have fallen; so now I brace myself, posture straight, chest flexed and eyes shut, as I leap. With each falter I have picked myself up from the ground and slowly brushed off the dirt.

Now my body feels worn down, and my legs feel too heavy to jump again. I am trying to push through the fatigue and take another leap toward my parents' acceptance. This time, standing beside me is Lily, my Lois Lane, who has reached out her hand and has placed it on my shoulder. I look back at her and realize I have been leaping toward a moment that I don't have control of, and all of the acceptance I need is standing beside me and around me.

My leaping days aren't through, but I know I need to move on to new buildings and new dreams.

EPILOGUE

FINDING MY GEMINI

My life consists of extreme emotions that fly from love and happiness to loneliness and depression, and back again. Leaps of faith can't exist without being able to survive the darkness. There are times where I feel less hopeful in the outcome, but I have refused to give up. I've been through too much in life to end it.

Since I was a child standing in the dark pastures, I had looked up to the stars in search for my happiness. I wished for my feminine skin to transform into the masculine twin. It's ironic to think I was born a Virgo, which is described as feminine and introverted. I've become the exact opposite, Gemini. I knew as a kid that the happiness had to come from within me, but I lost that awareness as a young adult, believing that others would have to bring me happiness.

My life has revolved around a haphazardly choreographed dance. One side of the dance troupe was composed of white figures; the other side was composed of black. Each dancer would rotate, turn, wriggle, and twist.

While intermingled the colors would crash, fall and trip, until they broke apart, lost on the opposite side before the process repeated itself. Through my struggles and fights surrounding my life and my relationships, I have found myself in a place where the dancers are now joined together as one being, with their bodies split by the colors white and black forming gray.

They still twist and turn, but they are never lost or alone.

I have now found a home in my body, a home in my relationship, and a home in my friendships with other people who are also on their own unique journeys.

I proudly climb upon the stage in this universe, waiting for my next move, and, hopefully, it will end in a standing ovation.

AFTERWORD

I am often asked why I continue to go out and share my story with complete strangers. I don't find myself even blinking when I respond with the following beliefs:

No person should be denied medical coverage because of who they are or how they identify.

No person should be fired from a job because they plan to transition or have a same-gender relationship.

No person should be kicked out of their home because they love someone of the same gender or are seeking help to align their body with their mind.

No person should be denied legal recognition of their relationship or children because they don't fit into the idealized view of what a relationship and family should look like.

No person should be left feeling alone, worthless, and nonhuman because they identify as LGBTQ.

I share my story because I believe that each person who is able to open up to the community will make a positive impact on how people are treated in the future. The number of suicides that we read about in the papers and the e-mails I receive from confused, lost, and lonely youth continue to propel me forward.

According to statistics provided by the 2007 Massachusetts Youth Risk Survey, "lesbian, gay and bisexual youth are up to four times more likely to attempt suicide than their heterosexual peers."[1]

Another research article "Suicide and Life Threatening Behavior" states that "nearly half of young transgender people have seriously thought about taking their lives and one quarter report having made a suicide attempt."[2]

I believe that if these statistics were related to heterosexual youth, there would be more funding and programming available to help families. But one of the problems is, home environments and family acceptance is one of the leading risk factors for suicide attempts and idealization by LGBTQ youth. Researcher Caitlin Ryan with the Family Acceptance Project has published multiple articles that all state in some form or another that "family acceptance of LGBT adolescents is associated with positive young adult mental and physical health."[3]

Isn't it amazing that families who give their children unconditional love, and provide them with a nonjudgmental environment to explore who they are, can have such an impact! Should we expect anything different from our families? The answer is "No."

This book wouldn't have taken form the way it has if it wasn't for the experiences that I've had in my life. The work I do as a public speaker, and the trainings I provide on LGBTQ inclusion in the workplace, medical setting, or on a university campus, wouldn't be as heavily needed if we could open up and respect the uniqueness that we all have as individuals. However, with all of the oppression, hierarchies, and judgment in the world, fully accepting environments are hard to find. So I'll continue on with my mission, and continue to educate diverse audiences on the complexities, as well as simplicities, that are related to a LGBTQ identity.

I don't see myself as a trailblazer, but I do see myself as a specialist. I am dedicating my life to improving environments for the LGBTQ community, with the hope that each person I reach will then impact another. My hope is that the ripple effect will allow us to see the ratio of LGBTQ youth who've committed, attempted, or idealized suicide reduce dramatically. No person should ever feel so much pain that he or she believes the only way to make it stop, is to make him or herself stop.

For those families that have lost a loved one to suicide, I hope that you will also reach out and ask for the discrimination against LGBTQ people to stop. I see changes happening every day, and most have been for the better. For those individuals who don't believe they have a future, I'm living proof that the world, although scary and sometimes draining, is a place that deserves your full-life exploration.

I just ask one thing of you: honor your truths and never compromise your identity, desires, and dreams. The greatest thing you can do for yourself is to let go of the fear and what-ifs in relation to your identity. They exist to hold you back, and you'll find that once you push past them, there is no stopping you.

You don't need a cape to fly. All you need is faith in yourself.

BIBLIOGRAPHY

1. Massachusetts Department of Elementary & Secondary Education. (2008). *Massachusetts Youth Risk Survey, 2007*. Massachusetts Department of Public Health.

2. Grossman, A.H., & D'Augelli, A.R. (2007). "Suicide and Life Threatening Behavior." *The American Association of Suicidology*, 37(5), 527-537.

3. Ryan, C., Russell, S., Huebner, D., Diaz, R., & Sanchez, J. (2010). "Family Acceptance in Adolescence and the Health of LGBT Young Adults." *Journal of Child and Adolescent Psychiatric Nursing*, 23(4), 205-213.

4. Halberstam, Judith. (2005). *In A Queer Time and Place: Transgender Bodies, Subcultural Lives*, New York University Press.

5. Stryker, Susan. (2008). *Transgender History*, Seal Press.

6. Long, Tony. "Dec. 1, 1952: Ex-GI Becomes Blonde Beauty." *Wired. com*. Conde Nast Digital, 01 Dec. 2008. Web.

7. Perez, Jr, Juan. "No Review in 'Boys Don't Cry' Case." *Omaha.com*. Omaha World-Herald, 26 Apr. 2011. Web.

8. *The Brandon Teena Story*. Dir. Susan Muska and Gréta Olafsdóttir. Zeitgeist Films, 1998. Documentary.

9. *Boys Don't Cry*. Dir. Kimberly Peirce. Fox Searchlight Pictures, 1999. Film.

10. Cameron, Loren. (1996) *Body Alchemy: Transsexual Portraits*, Cleis Press.

ABOUT THE AUTHOR

Ryan Sallans, born and raised in rural Nebraska, began his transition from female to male in 2005. He works as a public speaker, diversity trainer, consultant, publisher, and author specializing in health care, campus inclusion, and workplace issues surrounding the Lesbian, Gay, Bisexual, Transgender, Queer/Questioning, Intersex, and Asexual (LGBTQIA) community.

Today, he is most known as a national speaker who shares his transition journey, as well as his struggles with an eating disorder. His story is told with an intermixing of humor and intricate clinical details surrounding the transition process.

Ryan attended the University of Nebraska-Lincoln, where he received a Bachelor of Arts degree in English and anthropology, a Master of Arts degree in English, and a Master of Arts degree in educational psychology.

To learn more, visit Ryan's website: ryansallans.com.

ACKNOWLEDGMENTS

This book and my story wouldn't be what they are today without the love, laughter, and support, as well as hardships, tears, and struggles, I experienced with you, Michelle. I'll never take for granted the time we had; you'll always be in my thoughts. I bring the same sentiment to my siblings, Greg and Debra, as well as other family members. I know we all haven't seen eye to eye over the years, but something stronger has come through the heartache and the miscommunication on both of our ends.

My voice, my strength, and my motivation to continue have been inspired by my friends and by the amazing students and universities that invite me into their lives and into their classrooms.

No words can express the gratitude I have toward my friend and amazing photographer, Fred Schneider. You spent four years following me around in the wilderness and snapping away in your studio, in order to capture the eloquent images scattered among the pages. I feel indebted to my editor, Stephanie Finnegan, and designer, Erika Block, for helping me accomplish one of my childhood dreams, and college aspirations, to be a published author. I knew I couldn't do much with my B.A. in English, but the M.A. is a different story.

Finally, this book wouldn't have happened without the support from two amazing women in my life.

My former manager, Rosy Stefanatos—you gave me a new stage to use my voice and new opportunities to expand my professional image through your ongoing support and hard work.

My wife, partner, and best friend, Lily—every day I look at you and just want to breathe you in. I've never felt love like I do with you. You know when to push up against me and make me question my true feelings, and when to just stand beside me and let me feel. I'm prepared to weather any storm with you, I could lose everything else in life, but it doesn't matter, all I need is you.

Thank you for putting up with a guy like me.

CPSIA information can be obtained at www.ICGtesting.com
Printed in the USA
LVOW04s1733060715

445137LV00019B/1143/P

9 780989 586825